GOD CRAZY

Michelle Borquez

HARVEST HOUSE PUBLISHERS

EUGENE, OREGON

Cover by Koechel Peterson & Associates, Inc., Minneapolis, Minnesota

Cover photo © Larry Williams / Larry Williams and Associates / Corbis

GOD CRAZY
Copyright © 2007 by Michelle Borquez
Published by Harvest House Publishers
Eugene, Oregon 97402
www.harvesthousepublishers.com

Library of Congress Cataloging-in-Publication Data
Borquez, Michelle.
God crazy / Michelle Borquez.
    p. cm.
ISBN-13: 978-0-7369-1910-4 (pbk.)
ISBN-10: 0-7369-1910-4
1. Christian women—Religious life. I. Title.
BV4527.B66 2007
248.8'43—dc22

                                            2006030636

Printed in the United States of America

07 08 09 10 11 12 13 14 15 / VP-SK / 10 9 8 7 6 5 4 3 2 1

"Michelle Borquez's authentic compassion for others is both refreshing and inspiring. She herself has taken this adventurous road trip and has invited you to ride along and discover the joy that is available through surrender. I encourage you to take the risk, jump in, and enjoy the ride."

—JILLIAN CHAMBERS, co-pastor with husband
of Oasis Worship Centre, Nashville, Tennessee

"*God Crazy* will remind you that He is nuts about you! No matter what experiences have robbed you of self-esteem, destroyed your courage, shattered your dreams, or challenged your faith, God is on your side—cheering for you, encouraging you, and embracing you with the only love on earth that is perfect. Michelle is a visionary, passionate woman who will help you to develop a positive plan of action as you hold on to unshakable faith."

—CAROL KENT, speaker, author of
A New Kind of Normal

"The moment I met Michelle Borquez I felt easily connected to her, but most especially I felt that she connected with me. God has gifted her with discernment (and amazing class) to act as the ultimate filter for channeling information and experience into a message that could only be from Him! 'To God be the Glory' resounds through all she does and is!"

—LISA OSTROWSKI, president of
Women's Aglow Arlington

"Michelle Borquez is a powerfully dynamic and deeply authentic woman of God. She's been seasoned beautifully through the challenges of life. She understands richly the grace and mercy of God. I am always amazed when I have the opportunity to talk with Michelle and to hear her heart. It consistently cries out to the hurt and broken woman. Her life-changing message points us to the giver of all life...Jesus. He is the restoration and hope we all long for."

—TAMMY MALTBY, author, speaker,
and cohost of television's *Aspiring Women*

"I have been blessed by the burning passion of the *God Crazy* message that has emanated in Michelle over the years. The vision God has placed within her is inspiring and transformational. She is a great woman of impact."

—DR. CATHERINE HART WEBER, author,
adjunct professor Fuller Theological Seminary

To the many people whom God has used in my life to challenge me to become all He has purposed for me, thank you. To those who have been a great support to me as I have walked out the *God Crazy* life, I am indebted to you forever.

—Michelle

To my children: Joshua, Aaron, Madison, and Jacob. I sit back and am amazed at your wisdom and the way God is working in your lives. You teach me, you honor me, and you love me in such a beautiful way. I am thankful to God for the gift I have found in each one of you. I love you with all my heart.

—Mommy

God Crazy is dedicated to women everywhere, women whose light has slightly dimmed, whose heart has drifted a bit, or whose journey has been one of great challenge. There is more to our life than what we may realize. Embrace the God-crazy road trip and get ready for the ride. From here on out it's smooth sailing, girls, even in the midst of the storms!

❀ ACKNOWLEDGMENTS ❀

This book was inspired out of my own desperation to know God in a deeper way. To my amazing parents, Tony and Sandy Hormillosa, who pushed me to want this kind of intimate relationship and to settle for nothing less. You are the reason I long to be God crazy, and witnessing your example over the course of my life is what has challenged me to never accept a mediocre Christian walk. Your lives reflect the God-crazy life I desire to live.

I'd like to thank Carolyn McCready and Terry Glaspey of Harvest House, who have expressed their belief in me and this message over one too many dinners. You are more than friends... you are family. Thank you to Hope Lyda and all those at Harvest House who worked on *God Crazy*. You are the bomb. Thanks for pouring your heart out over this manuscript. David Dalton, I am thankful for your insights on surrender, thanks for your support as a brother in the Lord! To Ken Abraham for your words of encouragement and your advice as a fellow writer. Thank you for taking time out to lend a hand. To Dr. George Grant for inspiring me in the faith and in the Word and taking time to mentor me as a leader! Lastly, thank you to Bill Anderson who is an amazing support and a great encouragement in my life. You can't mess it up!

To my sister friends who are all God crazy, too many to name. Thank you for challenging me. I adore each of you. When I have been unable to walk, thank you for carrying me.

And once again, to each of my children: Joshua, Aaron, Madison, and Jacob. You are my treasures here on earth. You bless me and breathe life into me.

I love you all.

❈ CONTENTS ❈

In him we have redemption through his blood, forgiveness of our trespasses, according to the riches of his grace, which he lavished upon us, in all wisdom and insight making known to us the mystery of his will, according to his purpose, which he set forth in Christ as a plan for the fullness of time, to unite all things in him, things in heaven and things on earth.

Ephesians 1:7-9

You're Invited

They who wait for the LORD shall renew their strength;
they shall mount up with wings like eagles; they shall run
and not be weary; they shall walk and not faint.

ISAIAH 40:31

Close your eyes and imagine yourself in a field. There are no borders or boundaries around the field. It goes as far as the eyes can see. You are free to roam, dance, sing, laugh, run, have joy, or have pain, and nothing can touch you except for God. No one has access to you, your heart, or the desires and longings in your soul except for God Himself. In the middle of the field is a table with a narrow wooden frame that runs far into the horizon, as far as you can see. Fresh baked breads, fine meats, ruby-colored wine, lush fruits, and decadent desserts adorn the table. In the field are sunflowers in different shades of brilliant yellow, standing tall with their radiant faces covering you as if to protect you from the heat of the sun. While taking in the wonderful sight before your eyes, you hear God whisper, "This cannot compare to what I have prepared for you in heaven. It is simply a taste of all I have for you."

We may not have all heaven has to offer yet, but if we receive God's embrace, His passionate pursuit of us, then He will give us a taste of what is to come. But we must receive if we are to experience all He has to offer us.

> "The LORD is my shepherd, I shall not be in want. He makes me to lie down in green pastures, he leads me beside quiet waters, he restores my soul." *You guide me in the paths of righteousness for Your name's sake, and even though I walk through the valley of the shadow of death, I will fear no evil, for You are with me. Your rod and Your staff—oh, how they comfort me! You prepare a table before me in the presence of my enemies. You anoint my head with oil, and my cup overflows. Surely goodness and mercy will follow me all the days of my life, and I will dwell in Your house forever, Lord…forever. I will live with You, Lord, all the days of my life* (see Psalm 23).

At the very end of the movie *Braveheart*, William Wallace (played by Mel Gibson) says, "All men die, but few men really live." How true. All of us can get through this life, but how many of us will live it in the abundant way God intended? How many of us will dine at the endless table of His provision all the days of our lives?

Together we will explore the abundance and grace of this banquet table, because it is in this journey that we learn how God wants us to satisfy the hunger for meaning and love that has been a part of our lives forever. We're packing up for the road trip of a lifetime. I'm bringing prayers, God-crazy moments, and La Vida Loca (The Crazy Life) questions to help you embrace this fabulous, boundless new adventure. Together we will understand what the God-crazy life is and how it ushers us to the Creator's heart.

You're invited to the banquet of the Lord. La vida loca has begun—then again, it has been at the heart of your spirit all along. Let's start living it.

Run Through the Meadows Green

As we run through the meadows green
My spirit loves to hear You sing
I hear Your voice as I run and play
What will my Lord say to me today?

I dance in Your angels' light
And in Your shadow I shall hide
Let peace flow to me once more
As I dance in Your midst, my Lord

The oil of gladness pours over me
The wind and sea beneath
The music plays, it fills the air
And I no longer see

The veil between is far removed
In Your arms my soul be soothed
Nothing comes between us now
For today my Lord has saved me
Today my Lord has saved me

—Michelle

1

LONGING FOR MORE

*The LORD is near to the broken hearted and
saves the crushed in spirit.*

PSALM 34:18

Are we having fun yet?

Life—the Christian journey—should be infused with exploration and discovery and, yes, fun! God is untamed, unbound; there are no limits to what He will do in our lives if we are willing to let Him work through us and in us. God is mysterious and alluring and wants to reveal His mysteries to you. Do you wake up each day excited to experience what God is unveiling about Himself and His purpose for your life? It's a brave move to step onto an entirely new path and to awaken to your new life, but I guarantee it's worth it.

Are you ready to join me on an adventure on the open road of life? My friends tell me I bring a party wherever I go. Are you ready to join in on the party and have the time of your life? It's God's party and we are His guests, so let's sit back and let Him entertain us with all He has to offer! The only thing you are required to bring with you is yourself. Can you imagine a party where you are required to do nothing, bring nothing, and there is no cost to you at all, and what you get is the time of your life? You may be thinking, *Michelle, I'm not really that adventurous. I have so much to do, and hitting the open road sounds kind of radical. I'm getting used to just being here where I am. I don't see myself as ever having anything more or different.* Well, all that is about to change. I'm going to let you in on a big secret: Most of us go through our lives with the wrong impression about ourselves and our purpose. We don't "see" ourselves for who we really are intended to be in Christ. We look in the mirror every day, and the way we see that girl is not the same way God sees her. Our idea, our perception of all we think the Christian girl should be, may not be the true identity of what God wants for our lives. If we are constantly feeling that we don't measure up, that somehow God has set out a mandate for our every move on this earth, then we are living a life that produces striving and leads to exhaustion. I'd go even one further than that. Most of us spend our lives supporting, nurturing, and buying into the wrong impression and misdirection, so much so that we convince ourselves and everyone around us of this false version. We still work hard to maintain a sense that all is well, if not perfect, but we invest in a life that is far less than the one God designed for us.

> *We ALL hunger for love and attention and approval.*

Take a minute with that idea. Does that secret resonate within you deep down? Have you privately hoped and dreamed there is more to who you are and more to God's plan for your days? It's not easy to believe this great truth because we have a hard time letting go of what we are used to—even when it's a bad self-image. We might long for something different, but do we feel worthy of a life full of celebration and amazing, God-crazy moments?

Many of us look in the mirror and fail to see the woman God sees. What do you see? For many years I was paralyzed with fear and doubt about my value and even God's power to help me. I didn't have the ability to rise above the circumstances I had created because I had such a heavy sense of self-loathing. If you would have asked me to soar toward my gifting and my potential, I would have looked at you with absolute horror and defiance. "I can't," I'd say to myself and to others often.

We get so weighed down by the worldly version of living that we keep ourselves under the radar of anything good and empowering. My hope is that together we can get rid of all that limits you from complete, remarkable, exciting, God-crazy faith. Let's spend so much time soaring near the heavens that it feels like home. Let's reawaken and reacquaint ourselves with what Christianity was meant to be! Let's live the God-crazy life and show the world what it means to really be radical, confident in Christ, hopeful, and fun! We are created to rise above the everyday pressures of this life. The storms will come and trials will continue, but until we see ourselves as God does—capable, beautiful, significant, precious, and worthy—how we respond to and survive these trials will not change.

What We Believe

Our hard-held beliefs about our value alter our sense of reality early on. A few years back I led a Bible study for high school girls. One night during our devotion time I questioned them with "When you look in the mirror, what do you see? Do you see the beautiful girl God sees? What do you long for more than anything else?" I wasn't shocked to hear the answers I did, but I was surprised to hear the same response from all the girls. Not one saw herself as a beautiful gift, and they all longed to be loved and understood. They were uneasy as they discussed how defeated and unimportant they felt all the time.

We admitted that we felt insecure and that we often compared ourselves to others. Here I was with girls half my age, and yet we all had something big in common…we saw ourselves through a lens clouded by lies we believed about ourselves. This isn't a great revelation on its own, but the "why" becomes pivotal. Why do these girls and so many women feel unworthy or unimportant? The answer comes in the form of another question: "What makes us feel good about ourselves?" When I posed this question to the group, the girls shared how they felt better about themselves when a boy took interest in them. Shocker, right? How many of us still hunger for the adoring gaze of another person? Or praise from our parents? Or respect from strangers?

Most teenage girls can tell you what it takes to capture the attention or interest of a boy. This group, who was initially uneasy about sharing, jumped right into answering this question. With moony expressions, they revealed what it takes to pursue the giver of the attention they desire. Confessions emerged. They felt the effort and energy of being available, attentive, attractive, and appeasing were worth it if the payoff was validation from another.

They daydreamed of boys often and romanticized about how great they would feel if a certain one in particular liked them. If a girl is dating, she'll go on and on about how adorable the boy is, how she wants to spend every minute with him just to stare into his eyes and hold his hand. And she wants the same from him. She wants him to pursue her with phone calls, gifts, notes scrawled on crumpled paper between classes, whispered promises, text messages, modern poetic gestures of personalized music playlists, and unbroken gazes that take her breath away.

And she thinks of nothing else.

Boy crazy!

Yes. Completely boy crazy.

If it was too long ago to remember, or perchance you are one of the few women who never faced this phase of teendom, then let me reveal the underlying common denominator. We *all* hunger for love and attention and approval. Where we seek it might vary, but a huge void exists in all of us. We were created to long for fulfillment and communion and fellowship. We were created to seek God as the satisfier of our souls and the filler of that void. But throughout much of our lives we try to fill it with the wrong kind of love and satisfaction. Maybe your stand-in for true fulfillment is not a guy; you might be Success-crazy, Perfection-crazy, Power-crazy, Attention-crazy, or Security-crazy. The pursuit of everything and everyone except the true filler of our soul, the purposed completer of our heart, can go on for years and through many difficulties, letdowns, and periods of more self-loathing. It can go on so long that everyone else in our life might catch on to our patterns while we are still blind to them. What teenager sees straight when she is in pursuit of acceptance, love, and romance? But everything changes when we set out to discover the God-crazy life. It might be when you are at your lowest, when your heart is broken, when your stand-in has failed you (and it always does), or it might be when you are just plain tired of working hard to achieve a standard of acceptance and value that doesn't even match who you are on the inside. When we are consumed with God, we become passionate about the things He cares about and take on His big dreams for our lives.

But we cannot dream those dreams if we do not see ourselves as God sees us. We can never envision a life of greater depth and higher heights until we pursue God wholeheartedly and stop believing that voice inside us that tells us we are nothing until a man loves us or until we are popular, beautiful, successful, or applauded by our peers. We cannot embrace those dreams until we understand that the intended Pursuer of our heart and soul has been after us since before we were conceived. Our daydream of being loved by the One we adore is not fantasy but a full-on faith adventure.

My Journey to God Crazy

Being alone has never been something I've enjoyed, been good at, or wanted to do. I've always felt incomplete without a man in my life. Along my journey I had taken on the belief that I couldn't accomplish as much, or be whom God wanted me to be, unless I had someone to cheer me on and who showed me I was worth loving. The fairy-tale dreams we have as young girls stay with us. I, like many others, spent my girlhood dreaming of the perfect marriage, the children I would have, and the life I would live. I saw myself baking cookies, doing crafts, compiling photo albums with lots of marvelous family memories, and creating a home everyone would envy. This was the big dream I had for myself.

And for many years I thought I was living it.

But when the dream began to fall apart, when I began to see signs that my marriage was disintegrating, I did what Adam and Eve did when they found out they were naked...I covered up because of the shame. Instead of leaves from Eden, I used a busy schedule, a fake smile, conversations that implied life was normal, and preoccupation with my home and family.

Only my parents knew of the serious state of my personal life. Looking back, I know that if we had allowed people to be around us, God could have used them in mighty ways, and I would have been strengthened by their encouragement. But I was too ashamed. I was too embarrassed as a Christian to let others know I was in a place of crisis. Working to hold on to my image was exhausting. I was so worried about letting others down. I mean, "good Christians" know how to hold it together, don't they? I kept thinking I should be able to handle this on my own because I had the knowledge of God's Word, I was a leader in church, and I was a mentor to others. It's interesting that although my self-image was incredibly low, I still was convinced that I had all I needed to make this better—as if I could stare at all these ingredients and bits of my résumé more closely and they would create a remedy for this painful situation.

I'm not sure which was more tiring, making it seem as though my marriage was great to those around me, or making my husband happy and hoping somehow I could please him enough to make him love me. I thought if I was available, attentive, attractive, and appeasing I'd regain the object of my desire and the pursuit of my heart. Sound familiar?

This huge life disappointment triggered a huge faith crisis. I could not understand why God would allow this to happen to me. I'd been faithful, I'd served Him with all my heart, and now I was forced with a decision...to believe or not to believe. The dream I had been carrying all these years in my heart was now gone, and in its wake was a hole so deep, so wide, so frightening that I was sure I would never have a dream again.

I wanted God to come and rescue me from my pain. Without even realizing it, my anger and disappointment were beginning to be directed at Him. Where was He in my time of desperation? At this point in my trial I felt like Job when he tore his clothes and fell down on the floor, crying out to God in despair. "Where are You?" was a continuous shout from deep within my soul. I prayed and I begged my husband to go to counseling, only to hear him threaten me with divorce at the mere mention of professional help. I had done everything I knew to do, and still everything had crumbled down around me.

My world as I had known it was over.

The image of perfection I had worked so hard to maintain was slipping away right before my eyes. What would people think of me? What would my family feel? Who will ever love me again? These fear-building questions are what the enemy offers us in our time of weakness. "You aren't good enough and you never were. You are a loser, and now everyone will know the truth about you."

I had built up my own idea of what I wanted my marriage to be instead of seeing what my marriage actually was. I was holding on to the fantasy of a life fulfilled through another human being. Realization! I found myself in the darkest place I have ever been in my life. I have heard people say their divorce was like open-heart surgery with no anesthesia. I would completely agree. I don't think I've ever felt my heart hurt so deeply, my soul ache so intensely. I had failed God. Just as Peter had denied Him, I felt I had denied Him. I had sinned in so many different ways in my time of crisis. I had sinned in my heart, I had sinned in my thoughts, and I had sinned in my disobedience. I felt the enemy pressing me hard, pushing me to give up my faith, to just walk away. "Where is God when you need Him," he whispered to me. "He doesn't love you. He doesn't care for you." Listening to him, I felt myself slowly losing my footing as ideas of living the prodigal life once again enticed me, and thoughts of suicide filled my head.

My world as I had known it was over. I didn't want God. I was disappointed with Him, and I didn't want a book entitled *10 Ways to Fix Your Broken Marriage*. I felt I had read every book there was on marriage and had heard enough seminars to write a book myself. I wanted someone to hold me in my despair, to heal my wounded heart, and to love me in all the mess of my humanity.

Fortunately, I knew I needed to reach out. With great desperation, I called my friend and mentor Ruth Ann and asked her to meet me for breakfast. I was struggling with serious issues, and I wanted her to listen to what had become a five-year journey inward. I needed her to hear about my life and to speak wisdom into it as she so often had over the years.

Sitting at the local Cracker Barrel, with the hustle of the breakfast crowd all around us, Ruth Ann gently said, "Michelle, the picture you see of yourself is distorted. It isn't what others see, and it certainly is not what God sees. You are filtering everything through this version of yourself, and it is not truth. It's a complete lie." As I sat there nodding in agreement, my mind was racing with panic. I didn't know how or if I could get beyond this way of seeing myself and my existence. No matter how successful, no matter what accolades I had attached to my name, I couldn't see myself as someone God truly loved, passionately pursued, and tightly embraced. I felt like an outsider in my Christian journey, always trying to find a way to get in and to convince God I was His gal. Not only was I striving to prove to myself and others that I had worth, I was trying to convince God that I was good enough for His love. This was exhausting. Have you been there? If so, you know that no matter how hard you work or how fast you run, you *never* reach a point when you know you are good enough—that is, until you can receive God's goodness and His amazing grace. He does not ask for sweat equity before accepting you or me or anyone.

What's so interesting is that women generally extend plenty of grace to others in their lives. Most wouldn't dream of saying to a friend that she wasn't good enough for God's love or that she would never be pursued by her Creator. Yet when we turn our critical eye to that reflection in the mirror, the mercy stops, the grace dries up, and the perception becomes distorted.

I had held on to a false, lowly view of myself because I equated it to humility. I thought this endless mental list of my faults and problems would keep me from taking over the role of God in my life. And if I really kept up this self-bashing, I'd be sure to stay in God's grace and remain in relationship with Him. Well, I can tell you right now, the relationship I had with God was not the one He desired me to have with Him. The "grace" I wanted to stay within had nothing to do with God's grace and everything to do with worldly perfection and judgment. I was living in the Land of Opposite Thinking. I had everything wrong. Yet this bizarre world was comfortable and familiar. I was desperately hanging onto what I knew because I was afraid of falling from grace and turning back into the lost girl I was BC (before Christ).

The truth I couldn't see in that moment was that I had never stopped being that lost girl.

At breakfast that day, over plates of scrambled eggs, grits, and potatoes, Ruth began to pray for me to be set free. We held hands, and my friend spoke out this very simple prayer of freedom, and that was it. She looked at me with a stern look, and with authority in her voice she said, "Michelle, you are free."

"That's it? I don't need to fast for a year or be in a prayer closet for days begging God for freedom?"

"No, Michelle. The work was done on the cross, and today we have agreed and it is finished."

I felt a huge weight lifted. This burden I had carried for years was released. And though my full awareness of this and my ability to live in this new freedom took some time, in that moment I could see and feel God's love.

❀ GOD-CRAZY MOMENT ❀

I'll never forget the passionate African-American woman who came to my door one night when I was in one of my suicidal moments. Emotionally and physically drained from the depressive state I was in and feeling unable to cook, I had ordered pizza for the kids. When the knock on the door came, I was surprised to find it was not the pizza guy but a sales lady pitching magazines. She quickly explained that if she didn't sell enough magazines she wouldn't win the big trip to Jamaica. I quickly blurted out how I was newly divorced, broke, and definitely not able to help her. She immediately responded with her desire to pray for me. I couldn't believe my ears. "Okay," I feebly answered. I stepped out on the porch and this godly, obedient woman wrapped her strong arms around me and held me as she prayed. My kids gathered around and laid their little hands on my shoulders as they prayed along with her.

She belted out a prayer like you would not believe. She prayed exactly what I needed her to pray, even down to details no one but I knew about. With tears in my eyes, I hugged her tightly and thanked her from the bottom of my heart.

God had sent her to show His love for me. He pursued me. If I wouldn't go to church, He would bring church to me. Finally believing that God had not left my side is what finally broke my heart. I was so ashamed of my failure and still God pursued me with His unconditional love.

His Pursuit of Us

Who wouldn't be crazy about someone who loves us when we are the most unlovable, who loves us in the muck of it all, who comforts our heart in a moment of complete failure, or who covers us when we are disappointed? If someone treated you with such kindness and tenderness and wisdom, what would you do? You'd probably respond with the same level of love. You'd try to serve that person with equal care and concern. Not a day would go by that you wouldn't count your blessings to have a relationship so grounded in unconditional love.

This relationship awaits you when you turn to face your audience of One and pursue His heart completely. If you're like me, you've probably seen glimpses of what your connection to God could be like. It might have been during a troubled time, or it could have been amid a great, joyful celebration. The sense that you are loved deeply by the Creator is not meant to be a glimpse, a blip now and then during your life course. It's meant to be the nature of your ongoing journey with the Lord every day.

The only way to know God truly loves you and know He will pursue you is to take hold of the promises He gives you in His Word. I had head knowledge of Scripture and even a heart knowledge of God's truth; nevertheless, I had to experienced those promises at a point when the world had let me down, I had let me down, and there was only God to rely upon. I hope you won't have to get to this point to decide to book your ticket for the God-crazy adventure. In fact, why even wait a minute longer to wrap your mind, spirit, and heart around the fact that the Lord of all pursues you with a love you have craved since you were born?

Am I now seeking the approval of man,
or of God? Or am I trying to please man?
If I were still trying to please man,
I would not be a servant of Christ.
GALATIANS 1:10

The God-crazy message was birthed out of trial in my life. I made a God-crazy decision that I would no longer live my life for others, but I would live my life for Him and look upward for my validation and my direction. I would no longer live my life performing for others or striving to reach some standard that came out of misguided desires or expectations. Instead, I would allow God to work through me as a testimony of His mercy and grace. Living our life just for Him is not about being under scrutiny all the time or on some stage acting Christian for God. When we make God our sole and soul audience, then we are offering our lives, our actions, and our paths up to Him and His will. It is our action of surrender that gives Him pleasure. When we serve our audience of One, instead of an audience of many, we will meet our fullest potential.

How amazing it is to know that God pursues us even in our weakness and uncertainty. When we fail others or ourselves, it's difficult to believe we are worth loving. But if we look closely and see our image in the eyes of our single audience Member, then our hope rises up once again. We see our value, we see the One who shaped our purpose, and we know we are loved forever.

The God-crazy life is the difference between being motivated by obligation to serve others and serving because you are driven by love to share the mercy and abundance you have received. It's the difference between praying words and believing the words you are praying. It's the difference between reading the pages of God's Word as an observer and living out the words on the page as an adventure!

Are you feeling disappointed with the Christian journey you signed up for? Are you disillusioned because of difficulties you have faced? Do you feel deep down that there is more to Christianity than what you have experienced? Whatever brings you here doesn't matter because our inspired journey begins at this point. This is the miracle moment when a heart is prepared to open up to passionate, meaningful, transforming, adventurous faith. The God-crazy life will appear strange to the world and to Christians who hold on to their stand-ins. But for those who are daring, hungry, ready, and willing, the God-crazy life is the greatest adventure imagined (or even unimagined!).

❧ LA VIDA LOCA ❧

1. Have you felt a hunger for more purpose or passion or connection in your life?

2. When is the last time you let yourself think through your needs and longings? Do it now.

3. In what ways has your longing for love impacted your choices?

4. Has God raised you up out of a mess your pride created?

5. How often are you resting on your strength more than you are resting on God's power?

6. When was the last time you worried about what God thinks of a situation *before* worrying about what other people think?

7. How are you broken today? Where does this pain or shattered sense of self or love or purpose come from?

8. Looking back on your life, do you see ways God has pursued you? What are some of your God-crazy moments?

9. How would you define being "desperate for God?" Does it scare you to be desperate for anyone, even God?

10. God crazy is the difference between a life of limitations and a life of boundless possibility. Think through what that change can mean for your life today.

❧ GOD-CRAZY PRAYER ❧

*L*ord, *do not allow me to seek perfection;* instead, help me to yield myself to brokenness so that I might be perfected in You. When I forget that it's in Your power that I become clean and restored to wholeness, remind me. Lead me back to Your heart when I want to run off and do things my own way. Lord, help me to discover the ways I have hidden my brokenness even from myself. Give me the strength to sit with that realization and to seek Your mercy and guidance. Turn my longings for human approval into longings for Your grace and Your complete love. In Jesus' name. Amen.

2

JOYFUL SURRENDER

SURRENDER

My Lord, I offer up to You my life
A life so imperfect only You can purify
Come to me and quench this longing in my soul
I need Your living water to flow to me once more.
Let nothing, nothing, keep me from Your love
Because you are my Deliverer from all that I've come from
My Rescuer, my Righteousness, my Restoration be
For through You, and with You, I am finally free.

—MICHELLE BORQUEZ

Let's face it, the word "surrender" is a little scary. Our minds are programmed to think of submission and surrender as giving in or giving up. In this chapter and the next we will discover how far those misconceptions are from the truth.

If you have spent any time at all around kids, you probably have relied on the brilliant tactic of presenting everything as a game or adventure when they are either afraid or reluctant to do something. Well, this also works quite well on us too. (Have you ever told yourself that exercise is fun?) So come on, let's take a road trip. For those who enjoy being in a car for hours on end, "bring your pillow" is all I have to say. Surrender can be short and sweet, or it can be long and drawn out…depending on how tightly you are holding on to things.

I remember the beginning of my road trip to joyful surrender. It went a little like this: I was in the backseat of a car, the driver was masterfully maneuvering around obstacles at great speeds, my hair was stuck to the ceiling, my feet were planted firmly to the car floor, my hands were grasping tightly to whatever I could grab on to, my heart was racing wildly, and my thoughts were ranging from *Why did I get in this car?* to *Thank God I don't have false teeth because they'd be somewhere between me and the dashboard by now.* And even though the driver was calling out great sights for me to notice and commenting about side streets, I had no idea where I was going.

> *We forget that God wants something even better than what we want for ourselves.*

Can you imagine? Why would anyone jump into a car they had no control of and no idea where it was heading? And I'm pretty sure that any guidebook would advise that a tourist ask which direction the bus, subway, or taxi was going before getting in! But I had been driving myself and trusting only my driving for a long time. And the truth is, I didn't know where to go or what to do. I couldn't have called out the sights to anyone because my eyes were so focused on the horizon ahead, looking for a blaring sign to tell me "Michelle, go this way!" that I didn't pay attention to much else. I had tunnel vision and very little life vision.

So when I hit yet another detour that looked strangely familiar, I finally lifted my hands and flagged down God and said, "Can I have a lift?" You know what God must have been thinking when I asked that question? *Are you sure you are ready for the ride I'm going to take you on?* I'm glad I wasn't asked directly because I might have backed down yet again. Sometimes we are ready because circumstances usher us right to the intersection of our self-directed life and the God-directed life. Other times we are leaning forward, hands gripping the steering wheel, elbows out, eyes squinting, wipers wiping, and we just stop…weary, out of gas, and bleary-eyed from trying to read the small print of some man-made map.

Either timing is perfect. I encourage you to go for it. And this is the perfect opportunity. I'm here with you, and who doesn't love a road trip even more with a buddy along? We're in this together, and we've got the Master at the helm. All we need now are road trip munchies and a willing heart.

> *What no eye has seen, nor ear heard,*
> *nor the heart of man imagined, what God*
> *has prepared for those who love him.*
>
> 1 CORINTHIANS 2:9

First Stop: Surrender

We have learned to be in control of our lives. Surrender sounds as though we are headed the wrong direction, doesn't it? We like to stand in our own power and rely on our skills, abilities, and gifts to make our way. But the Giver of those very gifts asks us to surrender. Read this and then read it again: Emancipation begins when we embark on the road trip to joyful surrender. Our freedom is rooted in our belief in Christ and nothing else. We are not giving up control to someone we cannot trust; we are giving it to someone who has ushered us in and crowned us in His glory, a God who reveres us and loves us and the life ahead that is ours.

On the map that leads to surrender and ultimately to the God-crazy life, submission is the starting place. A friend shared these thoughts with me: "Michelle, people believe God is all-powerful. They just don't believe He loves them enough to do powerful things in their lives." This was so true for me. How about for you? We know God can do great things in our lives, but we don't believe He wants to do great things for us because we don't fully, completely trust that He loves us and wants the best for us. We carry hearts that have been disappointed by human versions of love. Our brokenness should make submission easier, but it can make us hard, disenchanted, and reluctant.

Every travel book will suggest that you pack the essentials and only those belongings that will enhance your travel, not those that will slow you down or become burdens along the way. I have a lot of friends who travel frequently for work, and they often rely on a checklist of what to take and even what to leave behind. After each venture they refine the list, and their load gets lighter and more efficient each time. If you've ever been slammed with an "over the weight limit" fee from an airline, you know how helpful this could be. The same is true for our upcoming trip. It will be easier and much more enjoyable if we are not battling with our baggage the entire way. We won't pay the high cost of lugging around hurtful and useless burdens, habits, and misconceptions.

Submission seems like giving up everything for nothing. We equate the unknown with a big, fat zero. Even if we don't love the situation, job, relationship, or goals we are in the middle of, we start to examine their worth in light of a scary exchange: Trading all these known factors for God's unknown will for our lives. We have the desires of our heart, and we worry that if we give the deepest part of ourselves to Him, those desires will be taken away.

Because we are still road weary from managing the trek alone, we forget that God wants something even better than what we want for ourselves. It's true! We think very small compared to the Creator. I didn't believe it for years. For so long I doubted that God would care enough about me to give me the desires of my heart or even bigger, brighter new desires. The deceiver likes us to remain afraid of God's best for us. When you are close to submitting, you will think God doesn't love you enough to take you places you are longing to go, or He won't let you bring along your kids, your husband, your relatives, and anyone else you love dearly, or that He will direct you toward a big dream and leave you stranded with only your own abilities. But once you start on the road to surrender and see how much peace it will bring you, you are going to want to bring others along, and then it will just get crazy fun because you will be out of control and God will finally be in control.

I have a friend who shared a great example of surrender with me. Years ago he was staying at a hotel on a business trip. He was in his room praying when he noticed an employee outside the window. He felt directed to talk with her, so he stepped outside into the fresh air and struck up a conversation. He had been in prayer quite awhile, and at this point he felt the presence of God and felt moved by the Spirit to show the light of God to this woman. (Don't try this unless you really feel it's God because, let's face it, girls, this could be a little odd if you don't feel confident God is speaking to you.) My friend spoke with this woman for a long time. He allowed moments of silence without feeling obligated to fill them. At the very end, he picked up a piece of wet clay from the area just beyond the sidewalk and molded it into a tiny heart, no larger than a thimble. He handed it to the lady and said, "This is your heart before the Lord right now. God is going to begin shaping it for you, just like I've shaped the clay."

Tears welled up in her eyes. He asked her if she would sell that heart for any price. He even reached for his wallet, but she shook her head no. He responded, "God has done a great thing today. If you had taken money in exchange for the clay, it wouldn't negate what He has done, but it would turn the heart shape back into just a mound of clay."

With a smile of joy she said, "My heart is the most precious thing I have. I will never sell it!"

A God-crazy woman will never sell her heart for any price because she has already surrendered it to the One who paid the ultimate price in death and resurrection. Your heart is the most important possession you have, and it is your offering to the Lord.

After I accepted a new life with Christ, it took me a little while to find my way. As a new Christian, I had superimposed my flawed worldview onto everything I did—something to understand, accomplish, and master. And for years I carved out routines in the Christian lifestyle, but when those routines revealed themselves to be too shallow and too narrow to uphold a true test of faith, I had nowhere else to go except to my knees. I was broken. And with my reservations down and my misconceptions of the Christian life crumbling all around me, I became hungry for God—His face, His Word, His heart, His life, His grace, His purpose, and His love for me.

My list of good deeds and best intentions might as well have served as a Kleenex to wipe away my tears at that point. They were useless for anything else. I didn't want to be formed by pouring my days into the Perfect Christian mold. I wanted to be transformed by pouring my heart and soul into the hands of the Creator. I wanted to submit to Him and to His mercy. I fell for God completely.

Anne Graham Lotz said to me once, "Michelle, God is a gentleman. He does not force His will on any of us." Surrender is about cooperative submission. God is not going to force you to take the road trip, nor will He force you to let Him drive when you do, but when your heart is ready, when you are tired of the road trips you have been on, He will be there waiting, holding the door for you, and He will wait for you to strap in.

Avoiding Potholes

The Christian life will not be a guarantee against rough patches. I'll bet you can attest to that in your own life. We've felt the sudden thud when the bottom of our world is dropping out from beneath us, haven't we? We know how our body shifts and shakes when we must swerve to miss a potential disaster. But even with some bumps along the way, you won't want to trade the road He takes you down for anything in this life. The more I have surrendered to all that this path requires of me and my faith, the more the Christian life has come alive to me. There are different kinds of potholes. Some are caused by the wear and tear of a life lived; others are caused by the elements—the rains that come with other people's actions and opinions and the harsh heat of unexpected trials which refine our faith and make it brighter. Still others are caused by our own actions. No matter the cause, we will feel these potholes, I guarantee it. However, if we can avoid making these divots in our own path, why don't we? Let's look at those personalities and behaviors that cause the most damage. If we address some of these at the beginning, the ride could be much smoother.

Backseat Driver

You can probably list a few of your friends and family members who fall into this category. Unfortunately, it is also a behavior that seems easy to adopt when it comes to our own faith journey. We get to a place in the Christian life where we begin to assume we don't need God's help. It might not be an intentional viewpoint, but we fall into the habit of directing our own life. Either we think we have learned enough about Him and His ways that we can call the turns and stops, or we feel we have waited too long to get where we want to go, so we shout out the directions we have jotted down on the back of an envelope that will lead to our next life milestone.

Whether we would want to admit it or not, we often have times when we look at God as a chauffeur who takes orders from us on where to go and when to be there. You'll find that this attitude often accompanies an overall sense of self-righteousness and judgment about others. If we consider the small percentage of people who actually are chauffeured from location to location, they tend to be people with plenty and who are able via finances and influence to direct others around. This is fame, not faith.

A God-crazy woman savors the freedom of letting God be in charge.

Shortsighted

"Let me off here. This is where I'm supposed to end up." We look out the window and point to the destination we are sure is meant for us. The ideal career, the family, the house with the gables and the contrasting trim, the ministry, the credentials that will serve as a passport to the good life. We are certain the road trip is over, so we jump out of the car. Suddenly a still, small voice asks, "Where are you going from here?" You stop dead in your tracks as you hear Him say, "I have more for you. More places to take you. I am not finished with you yet."

Surrender is a road trip that never ends. When we realize there is an ever-unfolding vision for our lives, then we know without fear of contradiction that we can trust Him because He truly wants the best for us. Our vision for our future and even for our present, everyday potential will be shortsighted unless we immerse ourselves in His Word and His eternal promises, and we relinquish the driving to Him. A God-crazy woman sees far enough ahead to live with purpose, but rather than gaze beyond the next step, she looks to her driver and says "Where to next?"

Perfectionist

Let's get something straight. Only the Lord is perfect. I know, I know...we think we are supposed to aspire to perfection, and a lot of us work really hard to attain it, but we are only *made* perfect through the blood of Christ; we can only see perfection when we look at the One leading us. He calls us to submission. He does not call us to put together the perfect birthday party or decorate the perfect house or design and carry out the perfect existence. Those pressures come from within and from others. Our quest for perfection is of God, but we misinterpret the meaning. Our quest is for perfection in and of Christ, not in addition to Him or outside of His grace.

I am guilty of striving for perfection. I always used to think it was all about being a good Christian. "Won't I show the world how great the Lord is when I succeed and when I prove to be extraordinary in whatever I do?" I thought I'd be a lousy witness if I was a complete failure every time I set out to do something. But that is the opposite of true. God's glory shines, His name is praised, and His grace abounds when we are flawed, human, broken, in need, and in submission to His power and His leading.

If every stop along your journey is not to your satisfaction, you'll miss the beauty of the view or a chance to get out and stretch, relax, and talk with God. If you are roving over some of those potholes and the ride isn't as smooth as *you* planned for it to be, it's the exact time you are supposed to rely on God for contentment, vision, and strength. A God-crazy woman surrenders her version of perfection and welcomes the opportunities to experience God's goodness and to lean on His understanding and perfect will.

White-Knuckler

Fear can keep us frozen in the backseat with our heart racing and our breathing shallow. When you are afraid of trials, of failure, or of the future, your energy will go toward survival and self-preservation. When your hands are tightly gripped around the door handle, you are not able to open them to receive what God is entrusting to you, nor are you able to give of the abilities and blessings you possess. The car might be moving, time might be passing, but you will be stuck in the same mode of worry. A white-knuckler spends all of her conversation time with God listing possible problems and praying for her version of a remedy. She doesn't often take time to listen for assurance or messages of hope and faith, and she certainly misses out on instruction. Believe me, what God asks of us can be simple, but it can also be scary, out of our comfort zone, and adventurous.

How many of us have faced financial difficulties or relationship troubles by plotting out how we will solve the problem? Much like a backseat driver, the white-knuckler is quick to voice her version of which way life should go, look, and feel. A God-crazy woman releases her grip on the handle, settles into the life God has given her, and breathes deeply. She knows that as wild as her adventure gets, she can rely on God's promises.

❀ GOD-CRAZY MOMENT ❀

I'll never forget driving down Highway 35 South on the stretch between Fort Worth and Austin, Texas. I had driven it several times during a troubled time in life as a means to escape my reality. This particular afternoon was no exception. I was so numb. The enemy began to taunt me. "Drive off the road. In one moment you can end it all. What is there to live for?" I began to entertain the thoughts and was seriously contemplating listening to the hopelessness when the phone rang. It was my dear friend Tammy. "Michelle, I don't know what you are going through, but the Lord put you on my heart today, and He has a word for you. He sees your pain, He has seen the unjustness of your situation, and He is going to redeem this in your life. Michelle, I hope I haven't overstepped my bounds. I just had you so heavy on my heart."

In that moment, I knew God was going to see me through. Tammy knew nothing of my situation. She didn't know my husband and I were in the middle of a divorce. She had heard the word of God and obeyed. She said one more thing to me after I told her my circumstance. "Michelle, God is going to use you to minister to women who have gone through similar circumstances…you will minister again." I thanked her for her willingness to call me and assured her she had not overstepped her bounds. I shared with her how at that very moment I was contemplating the idea of running my car off the road, and she was grateful she had called…very grateful.

Giving Your All

I remember a hymn from church as a small girl. This song, while written more than a hundred years ago, still resonates our faith today. Many of you will recognize these lyrics:

All to Jesus I surrender
All to Him I freely give
I will ever love and trust Him
In His presence daily live

I surrender all
I surrender all
All to Thee, my blessed Savior
I surrender all

This song paints such a true picture of surrender. I never really thought too much about the song itself when I sang through it as a young girl, but it always brought tears to my eyes and focused my heart on Jesus and His love for me. As an adult, I now recognize that what evokes such strong emotion in me with each verse is the word "all." Repeating it over and over throughout the song impacts my heart. The significance of all, everything, all of me, is powerful. It is surrender of every part of me, my life, my soul, my path, my hopes, my heart.

> *Don't be holding on to anything when you are praying a prayer of surrender.*

Most people associate surrendering to God as Him putting a clamp on your life. They worry that submitting our all to the Lord means we stop having a life. Just the opposite is true. We start living fully and intentionally when we surrender! " 'I know the plans I have for you,' declares the LORD, 'plans to prosper you and not to harm you, plans to give you hope and a future'" (Jeremiah 29:11).

Eight Keys to Surrender

I want to share a few keys I've learned in my life when it comes to surrender. There is no formula, but I do think there are ways we can open up to the act of surrender. Surrender is so removed from our vocabulary in today's culture that we need to learn what it means in the context of faith and the God-crazy journey.

1. *Surrender by its nature is unconditional.* You don't come to God and say, "I'll surrender this part of my life if You'll do this or that." That's not surrender. That's negotiating a contract with Him. We have covenant with God through the sacrifice and resurrection of His Son. We do not come to a bargaining table with Him if we are ready for abundant living. The faith relationship based on surrender does not start out with a prenuptial arrangement.

2. *Surrender is of the heart, not the head.* You can't just mentally agree that you need to surrender to God. You know in your heart what means most to you besides God Himself. That's a good place to start when surrendering.

3. *Surrender is done while kneeling.* It's good for the soul to pray a prayer of surrender on your knees. This is a position of humility. Your heart and head will be more in touch with the act of submission if your body also reflects this state of being. And I encourage you to do it by yourself, with no distractions. Surrender is between you and God alone.

4. *Surrender is done with both hands in the air.* You can't be holding on to something with one hand (like bitterness…or the door handle!) and praying a prayer of surrender with the other lifted. Don't be holding on to anything when you are praying a prayer of surrender.

5. *Surrender is dropping your weapons.* We arm ourselves with jealousy, bitterness, gossip, stubbornness, envy, and many other modes of spiritual destruction. Be willing to lay your human forms of self-protection at the foot of the cross if you are going to pray a prayer of surrender.

6. *Surrender is giving up what is good for what is best.* In our human version of an exchange, we give up something and get something of equal value in return. If we are people of justice, we want a win-win situation. When we fall for God, completely, and enter the realm of God crazy, we will discover that God goes so beyond our hopes. We might be willing to settle for that which is good,

or good enough, in our lives, but our heavenly Father wants that which is best for us.

7. *Surrender is a gift from God back to God.* God loves to give gifts to His children, but sometimes a gift from God can become an idol in our life—career, love, money, etc. God blessed Abraham with a son at a point in Abraham's life when he was certain he would never experience the joy of family. You can imagine how precious that child, Isaac, was to his father. When God called Abraham to sacrifice this beloved son, Abraham was in a relationship of surrender and was willing to do what God asked. The Lord honored Abraham's submission by releasing him from the obligation and giving him an alternative way to honor God.

8. *Surrender is done at the altar.* I don't mean a physical altar, but the spiritual altar of your heart. The altar is a sacred place and not to be taken lightly. It is a place of reverence. When you are praying a prayer of surrender, be mindful of the condition of your heart. Are you cloaked in humility? Are you making an offering that is pleasing and worthy of God's presence?

Are you ready to let go of good enough to embrace God's best? If not, list your worries and then pray through them. Our journey continues, and you won't want to miss one minute of it. Haven't most of us waited long enough to feel the wind in our hair, the smile of pleasure on our lips, and the joy of giving our all to God's very best? Let's ride on, friend.

⚜ La Vida Loca ⚜

1. How have you thought of surrender in the past? Do you believe you have surrendered fully to God?

2. When you think of trading your known life for God's unknown will, how do you feel?

3. What stands between you and full submission to your Creator?

4. Which personalities/behaviors are causing potholes in your road to God's purpose?

5. How do you plan to rid your life those behaviors?

6. Have you believed that a God-crazy surrender would stifle your life and hinder your happiness?

7. Read the verse of "I Surrender All." Reflect on how it feels to say and mean the word "all."

8. Do you believe that surrender and submission are acts of joy? Consider how light and relieved you will feel when you give your all to the God-crazy life and receive absolute freedom to love the Lord, follow His plan for you, and embrace a much bigger and better version of abundant living than you have ever dreamed possible.

9. Take time to go through the eight keys to surrender in this chapter. Feel the power of falling to your knees, lifting your hands in praise and submission, and letting go of destructive patterns.

10. Go to the altar of your heart and lay down material possessions, fears, bits of pride, past hurts, and everything else that comes between you and the Lord. Envision placing each of these things in front of God. See His pleasure and His love for you.

❧ GOD-CRAZY PRAYER ❧

Oh, Lord! I am so ready to live differently and to feel the freshness of a new purpose and path. Give me the courage and the insight to figure out all that has kept me from surrender in the past and in the present. Lead me to the altar of my own heart, where I can take time to pray and to release my hold on the world's version of living so that I can grasp hold of Your adventure for me. It is exciting to know that You have a plan for my life, and that You see me as Your precious child. All to Thee, my blessed Savior...I surrender *all*. In Jesus' name. Amen.

3

THE NATURE OF SURRENDER

Without faith it is impossible to please him, for whoever would draw near to God must believe that he exists and that he rewards those who seek him.

HEBREWS 11:6

I wouldn't be a very enjoyable fellow traveler and God-crazy companion if all I talked about were the potholes behind us and nothing about the beauty, wonder, and fascinating view ahead of us. Surrender will surprise you by its many different characteristics and mighty power to change your life, perspective, and direction with godly force. I'm always telling my kids "Everything in moderation, except God" because as we make our way in this life, we should seek God with every bit of our desire and strength. As a result of this complete submission, God fills us, covers us, and leads us to the abundance of surrender. The way you look at each day, each person, and your own heart will never be the same when you experience the full nature of surrender.

The Swiftness of Surrender

Hoover Dam, one of the largest dams in the world, is located in the vast desert of Nevada. At select times of the year, millions of gallons of water from the Colorado River come pouring out into a riverbed, where it is guided for irrigation and power. The water is directed for an important purpose: It brings life to the desert and parched areas. What an incredible metaphor for what God does when He begins to pour His Spirit and love into our life. It is not haphazard. His love has a direction. It quickly fills your heart to connect you to Him and then to others. The divine flow of God's love seeps in all the nooks and crannies of every area of your life just as the water released from the Hoover Dam rushes around and over rocks and soon completely covers what was dry, unfruitful ground. Be assured of one thing, when you surrender, God's love and the power of that love is not going to be a like a leaky kitchen faucet trickling into your life. Surrender's joy will swiftly fill your soul, bring life to the desert of your former self, and bring to the surface His gentle and loving handiwork in all the details of your life.

When we have truly surrendered all, God can work quickly in us and through us, so much so that we usually will see evidence of His presence right away. I remember when I surrendered my dream house to God. We had put an offer on a beautiful house after many years of living in an apartment with two kids. I really wanted this house, but I knew God would see beyond my immediate hopes to the bigger plan He had for me and my family. So I surrendered the outcome to Him. I prayed and released my desires for this house to God, and within a day I felt a strong sense that the house should not be our home. The house seemed perfect, but I knew God must know differently. So we pulled the contracted offer. Later that same week we found out we were being transferred to Denver and would need to move within a month. What a relief. I was so thankful we had not bought that house. What a mess we would have been in! Though we can't know everything in advance, God sees into the future, and He knows what is best for us if we will trust Him.

The Solitude of Surrender

In one of my favorite movies, *Castaway,* Tom Hanks gives an extraordinary performance as an executive for a delivery service whose plane crashes into the sea during a storm. He survives the crash and is left in the middle of open water without any way to know where he is. Finally he makes it to an island, and as a viewer you are relieved for him to find land, but, of course, true survival and a test of his character and will is just beginning. Much of his will to survive centers on being reunited with his girlfriend. Her photograph inside a locket is in front of him every day as a reminder of what he has to live for and fight for during his time of loneliness and fear. He endures many hardships, setbacks, and failed attempts to leave the island, but through it all he remains faithful to his sole purpose. When he is finally rescued and back in the highly superficial world he once knew, you sense that he wouldn't change the last 1500 days of his life for anything. Interestingly, he doesn't seem to be judgmental about the overabundance; instead, you can see that he feels sad for the people he formerly associated with and their blindness to what really matters in life. He becomes just as determined to find his new purpose in his new life as he had been determined to survive the dangers of the island.

This character does not surrender to hardship and give up, but he does surrender to the work it takes to become a better, stronger, and more purposed person. What a transformation he makes during his time of complete solitude. Surrender can be a lonely place. It can feel as though you are on an island far from what you have known before and far from how others live. Don't expect a ticker tape parade down Broadway. Many people will not see what God is doing in your heart. To see someone truly surrendered to God unnerves some people, regardless of how normal you might try to act. Some people will see your heart of surrender as a weakness and be inclined to make comments such as "Can't you just make your own decisions?" or "God gave you a mind to use on your own."

You might have times when you feel very alone on the highest peak on that distant island, but this is where surrender leads you: to the rescue of God's presence. Jesus lived a surrendered life. His will was surrendered to His Father's, and He wasn't always well received, but He was resurrected in the very power of His Father.

Recently, I went to see a movie with a friend. It seemed like it would be a hilarious comedy based on the clips shown, but when we were in the theater and the film began, I realized quickly that it was highly offensive. I was shocked at how degrading it was toward women, and it didn't stop there. It went on to degrade Jews, marriage, and on and on. I was grieved and knew I had to leave this movie. I didn't want to drag my friend out and act as though I were his moral compass, so I excused myself and went to wait in the lobby. Within moments my friend was sitting next to me. I shared my feelings of grief over what I had seen and how I could not sit in a movie that so blatantly mocked human dignity. His response surprised me. He felt I was overreacting, and he did not agree with my sense of the film.

> Here's the great irony: Surrender is the ultimate freedom of choice.

Several weeks later he had a life-changing experience with the Lord. I could see that he had surrendered his heart to God, and one of the evidences of this was his admittance to being insensitive to my grief over the movie. He also admitted that he had not been careful about the movies he rented for his teenage son to watch. His heart was broken over his lack of discernment. My point is this: Many times people take offense at what offends you. Usually it will only be those who have surrendered to God's leading and sensitivity who will be able to fully empathize.

When we surrender, we see God's creation for what it is, the very image and creation of His. It will pain us when that creation is trampled on by harmful and hurtful actions, comments, and attitudes. When we stand for discernment, there will be times when we stand alone.

The Security of Surrender

Jim Elliot, a martyred missionary, wrote in his journal: "He is no fool who gives up what he cannot gain to gain what he cannot lose." This is one of the divine paradoxes of surrender. When you let go, when you give up, and when you finally give in...then you feel a supernatural security that can only come from God. It isn't giving in to pressure or giving up to an enemy; it's the giving over of your will and your present and your future to the King of kings. In our fallen nature we think we can make a better choice than God. All around us we hear the virtues of having a freedom of choice. In the '60s, the women's movement was focused on freedom of choice and opportunity. While there was some truth behind the need, movement leaders and those who participated in the collective voice of the time were going about it with anger and vengeance. Here's the great irony: Surrender is the ultimate freedom of choice! And it can never be born out of a heart of rage. You choose to surrender to God. What decision in this world could be wiser than choosing the way of our all-knowing God? Who knows what's better for your life than the Master Designer of all life?

The Sacredness of Surrender

Do you own any family heirlooms that are priceless? When my grandmother died recently, she left very little behind. She had given away most of her belongings before she passed away so she could see her children benefit from what she gave to them. Among the few things she left behind was a collection of bells she had bought at different times in her life. Each bell represented a time or place and had special meaning to her. While living, she always had them lined up on a shelf over her doorway, nicely displayed for all to see. When she died, my mother gathered up all the bells so she could have them as a reminder of the wonderful memories she had with her mom. I asked my mom if she would mind if I also took a couple to remember my grandmother by. I am so sentimental, and my granny was one of the most important women in my life. She handed down to me so much spiritually and personally; I knew these bells would be a reminder of all she meant to me over the years. Mom gladly gave me a couple of the delicate bells, and they now sit in different places throughout my home. I am sure when people see them they may wonder why I have a bell displayed that does not fit the character of the rest of my decor, but it doesn't matter. These bells are priceless to me and will always remain somewhere nearby. The priceless heirlooms of the heart which my grandmother passed along to me will be even closer.

When you hold a surrendered heart, it's the most precious possession God could have ever given you. It's like a sacred white pearl straight from your heavenly Father. There are many things we gladly inherit when we become a Christian, but a lot of Christians have not yet discovered the value of the surrendered heart, so they remain distant from it. They might examine it from time to time but are undecided about what purpose it serves or what value it will have in their Christian walk. By the time we are through this journey to God-crazy living, you'll be able to tell them and show them exactly how a surrendered heart makes the journey worth taking.

Remember the story of my friend giving the heart-shaped piece of clay to that woman? That bit of insignificant, dried-up clay turned into a precious and sacred heirloom once placed in this woman hands—it represented her heart. That small portion of the earth is a sacred symbol of her heart's surrender to her heavenly Father. Hold on tightly to such symbols, as they are precious reminders of the decision you have made, but never let the symbol become more important than the state of surrender.

The Supernatural Side of Surrender

What do I mean by supernatural? Simply that none of us has the natural ability to have a God-crazy surrender. You can't do it apart from God. You can't stop living for yourself in your own might, but only through the power of the resurrected Christ. If you try to do it in human strength, it will wear you down and wear you out quickly. When you feel that this life is too overwhelming to do alone, embrace this feeling! See this feeling as your friend. It's your tutor leading you to Christ. Your inability to surrender is, at this point, made known to you by the Spirit of God.

> *And he died for all, that those who live*
> *might no longer live for themselves but for*
> *him who died and rose again on their behalf.*
> 2 Corinthians 5:15

It is not by fulfillment of your will, but by a surrendering of your will that authentic Christian living can begin. If you or I were able to clean up our act by the force of our will, as opposed to the grace of God, we would probably experience a self-righteous attitude, a prideful heart, or a misguided next step. Those basking in self-righteousness are playing into the enemy's hands! Self-righteousness grieves God, turns others off, and disintegrates a person's sense of priority and empathy.

Acknowledge to God you can't surrender in your own strength. That's your first step to surrendering!

The Sweetness of Surrender

"Six days before the Passover, Jesus therefore came to Bethany, where Lazarus was, whom Jesus had raised from the dead. So they gave a dinner for him there. Martha served, and Lazarus was one of those reclining with him at the table. Mary therefore took a pound of expensive ointment made from pure nard, and anointed the feet of Jesus and wiped his feet with her hair. The house was filled with the fragrance of the perfume" (John 12:1-3).

This is truly one of the most powerful passages in the Bible. Take a moment to reread it. A message is here for all God-crazy women who will embrace it. Did you know that this perfume Mary poured out for her Lord cost close to a year's wages in that day? If we spent $100 on a bottle of perfume, we would consider that to be expensive. Imagine if a bottle of perfume cost $25,000? People would think you were crazy to spend so much. And if you removed it from its special place in your home and liberally poured it out over a person's feet…even your family would want to take you in for psychiatric evaluation. And you know your best friend would be saying, "Don't waste it on Him. Give it to me, girl!" Mary gladly sacrificed something of the world to honor the One who gave her new life.

Of all the women Jesus could have allowed to kiss His feet, to anoint Him for His burial, He chose a woman who had lived a woefully sinful lifestyle, a woman out of whom He had cast seven demons, a prostitute. Jesus knows everything; He knew who she was and what she had done. He knew how she had seduced men out of their money and used her body to cause many to commit adultery. But He also knew something far more important about Mary than her past. He knew she was a broken and surrendered woman, and He knew where He wanted to take her. He had forgiven her of her sins. His sweet words, "You are forgiven," cover all of our sins too. Surrender requires us to give all to Jesus, and His blood covers all that we are and were and will be—including the sinful nature. Have you heard these sweet words whispered to your spirit? If not, they are there! If so, did you believe them with every bit of your being?

God-crazy woman, let this sink as deep into your spirit as you are able: Your past is forgiven. If you are a surrendered woman, you will find yourself at the feet of Jesus, pouring out "the pure nard" of your heart, showering His feet with your tears, and oh, what an incredibly sweet aroma will fill your home and heart. People around you will sense the aroma of His presence in your life. This is what sweet surrender is like.

There is no place in your Christian walk where you will sense this "sweet aroma" more than when you are living and loving from a surrendered heart. This is truly the sweetest place to be in Christ.

Surrendered sweetness is an enduring joy that will not fade, and our Father has it there for you…come to Him with heart in hand and surrender.

Counterfeit Surrender

Okay, get ready…Michelle is about to burst some bubbles here. I'm not talking about your bubble, I'm talking about my own. I'm about to confess a shortcoming of mine, and if you think less of me, well, I'll just have to live with it. That is the cost of being honest.

I love shopping in New York, Chicago, or any big city.

You might be thinking, *Um, Michelle, that's hardly a major confession.*

Well, let me tell you why I like to shop in big cities: Sidewalk vendors. And more specifically, I love it when I come across the people who are pedaling counterfeits of my favorite brands. Every high-end brand name in women's accessories you can think of is represented. Now, this practice is tolerated in our country but frowned on by the *Devil Wears Prada* group…are you with me?

But I can't help myself. If we get to meet sometime, your eyes will now probably go straight to my purse, and you'll have visions of me buying a faux Gucci on a New York street corner. I can tell you right now, unless it was a gift (and I do love gifts), nine times out of ten I got whatever I have on or am carrying at a sale, on consignment, or on city streets. I just let you in on one of my greatest secrets. Now I can call you a friend for sure!

Yes, I know, the stitching is different, the leather is different, and the logo is sometimes different, but I always look for the absolute best copies to buy and pretty much know right where to go. I love it when I run into a friend and she lets me in on her bargain deal, don't you? So, once in a while I'll pick up the purse, the sunglasses, the billfold, etc. Now I can walk around as though I've got the real thing, smiling because I didn't have to spend real dollars! So, in my Christian humility, I'm hoping someone says to me, "Oh, what a beautiful purse. I can see it's a fake, but you must be a frugal

Christian woman and therefore your pride would not allow you to spend that much money on the real thing." Okay, maybe not. Truthfully, I am hoping no one knows the difference except God, a few buddies, and now you! Even though choosing counterfeit versions is not a life-altering risk, there is nevertheless a risk when doing so. Just the other day I noticed that a recent purchase was starting to tear and fade. Too bad for me because I can't take it back.

There are other counterfeits where you can go to jail. In the movie *Catch Me if You Can,* Leonardo DiCaprio plays a man who counterfeits being a pilot, a lawyer, and a doctor. He also counterfeits checks. He is caught and goes to jail. He was able to have this deceitful life for many years because he became so successful at pulling it off. The man the story is based on eventually worked to catch counterfeiters because he knew all the tricks to making something look as close to the real thing as possible, making the counterfeit difficult to detect.

So, what does counterfeit surrender look like?

Counterfeit conversion is also difficult to detect. This takes place in a person who has fooled themselves into thinking they have surrendered their heart to Christ. In talking to thousands of people across the country, I have found that many women and men are plagued with this false state of the heart. We are discovering that surrender is an ongoing journey. However, there is an initial point of surrender that we know in our hearts has been made. From that starting line of submission onward, we understand that we are going through a process of transformation that requires us to give ourselves and all that we do over to God's care. If a person has a counterfeit conversion, they might look and act like someone who has faced the real deal, but eventually the fabric of their faith will begin to tear and fade.

My oldest son, Joshua, recently said to me, "Mom, I've got friends who wear a different mask at school than when they are at church." My insightful boy was very disturbed at the lack of authenticity in others, and yet I am sure if he really looked at himself, he may find that he also wears masks at times just like his friends. It is unavoidable to refrain from mask wearing, but definitely easier with a surrendered heart.

Unfortunately, much of this mask wearing is picked up at home. Trust me, children spot hypocrisy a mile away, especially when those closest to them try to get away with it. Ya can't fake it at home, girls! I recently read that the Latin root word for "hypocrisy" means "to pretend or play a part." This term was originated from the theaters of Greece, where they would wear masks and alter their voices to play various roles. When I speak of masks, I'm not talking about changing your mind or having different moods (don't we all!). I'm talking about the times when you sacrifice the integrity of your heart by showing a revised self to the world when you have a deep faith. If you play a role, you are going against the authenticity a surrendered heart requires.

So, what does counterfeit surrender look like? Consider this well-known phrase: "You are saved by faith alone, but saving faith is never alone." Saving faith is a faith that reflects a surrendered heart. Think back to when you first asked Jesus into your life, what you might call your born-again experience or the day you accepted Christ. After the excitement and the feelings wore off, usually after a couple of weeks or months, what happened with your commitment? Did your commitment ride the same wave of highs and lows as your feelings? What happened when the good feelings wore off? In the parable of the sower, found in Luke 8, Jesus said (and I'm paraphrasing), "If you don't understand this foundational parable, how can you understand anything?" Jesus spoke of the person who initially received the word with joy. "The ones on the rock are those who, when they hear the word, receive it with joy. But these have no root; they believe for a while, and in time of testing fall away" (verse 13). This does not mean fall away in terms of your belief in God or Christ. Jesus is talking about falling away in terms of your surrendered life. Maybe you decide to take your life back into your own hands or slide into old, bad habits even after hearing the joyful word of the new way. People who have had a counterfeit conversion usually take a wheelbarrow full of previously seen sin to God once every six months and ask Him to forgive them.

A surrendered heart craves daily relationship with the Lord.

When a surrendered heart loses communion with God, it doesn't stay that way very long. It can't! I know this can be scary stuff and cause you to question yourself and your very salvation, but that's okay. I've got a friend who thought he was saved when he was eight years old, and after several rededications he finally realized that he had never truly surrendered. Only God can show you this in your heart, but don't fall into the trap of mistaking a great "God feeling" to really making a decision to surrender your life to Him. If you are not sure, then fault on the side of caution. If the Holy Spirit is tugging on your heart at this point, then it's because this word is for you.

If you are feeling that tug, then follow it. Take a moment to sing through all verses to "I Surrender All." Hold your hands up to the Lord as a physical manifestation of your desire to surrender. When you have finished, kneel down and take a moment to pray this prayer of surrender:

> *Dear Father, thank You so much for shedding Your light in this dark area of my soul. I've lived a life with so much frustration, so much double-mindedness, so much going back and forth in my surrender to You. I make no excuses for what has happened. I know You don't expect perfection from anyone, but this is not about perfection; this is about truly surrendering my heart and life to You. I repent for not truly giving my life over to You. Today, I make this choice. I need Your grace to help me do this. In Jesus' name. Amen.*

The Fruit of Surrender

Since you are reading this book, you are most likely at one of two places in your personal journey: You are either at a fork in the road and considering the road to surrender, or you are already on your way. Women at both places want to know what fruit their lives will produce after they choose surrender. I asked the same question. My simplest and purest answer: Surrender exhibits the character of God, the fruit of the Spirit. God's character is love, joy, peace, patience, kindness, goodness, faithfulness, gentleness, and self-control. These become the outward evidence of a surrendered heart. We are only capable of bearing this fruit if our heart is in a place of joyful surrender.

Joyful surrender comes from a very pure love for the Lord and the knowledge that we can trust Him. For some the joy blossoms by trusting Him for small things, others start out trusting Him with everything. It's up to us. The journey awaits us, and I will testify to you this journey is one you will never regret.

The fruits of walking in the flesh are impurity, sexual immorality, idolatry, sorcery, enmity, strife, jealousy, fits of anger, rivalries, dissensions, divisions, envy, drunkenness, and other destructive behaviors. These are all things we must throw out along the road trip, but all things that can only be released when we have completely surrendered to God.

Surrender is something we must look at every day. Even though we make the ultimate surrender of our all in all, we will still find ourselves from time to time asking God to put on the brakes or take a different turn. This fear or resistance is all a part of the process of learning to trust Him and His love for us.

❧ La Vida Loca ❧

1. Have you seen God move swiftly in an area of your life that you surrendered?

2. Which areas are the hardest for you to turn over to Him? Why do you think that is?

3. What does the solitude of surrender mean to you?

4. Think on how good it will feel to have the security of surrender. What might change in your life with just this one aspect of surrender?

5. Have you embraced the sweetness of the words "You are forgiven"?

6. In your life you have known those who are saved and those who are surrendered. What are the biggest differences? What do you want to model from those who are surrendered?

7. Which masks do you wear most often? Why do you think you started wearing masks?

8. Do you think you might have had a "counterfeit surrender"? If so, why?

9. What would be a symbol of your surrendered heart?

10. How have you witnessed the fruits of surrender?

❧ GOD-CRAZY PRAYER ❧

One True God, help me to seek an authentic belief and be open to embracing the nature of a surrendered life and faith. Break down the barriers I have built up. I cannot do this in my own power; I can only experience freedom through You and the flood of Your love and mercy. Your love reaches the parched places in my soul, and You bring new life. I'm excited for what the future holds when You hold my future in Your hands. I praise You and thank You for awakening me to a deeper faith. In Jesus' name. Amen.

4

A BETTER VIEW
UP AHEAD

*Faith is not about pretending our circumstances
don't exist, but rather admitting they do exist and
seeing beyond our circumstances into the realm of great
possibility for a miracle to occur. Faith is immersing
ourselves in hope and belief and wonder.*

—MICHELLE BORQUEZ

I love to road trip during the changing seasons—especially from winter to spring. The sun begins to shine a little longer, the flowers begin to bloom, and everything around me is fresh and new. When you leave behind your emotional or spiritual winter, there is a fresh view ahead, and it is filled with the color, fragrance, and life of spring—the God-crazy life is a new season, a new beginning, a stirring of sorts.

A dear friend, Linda Pearson, wrote these beautiful words to my mother:

The ebb and flow of My presence is not a sign of disgrace.
It's simply the process of My purpose as you run this spiritual race.
Keep your eyes focused upon My face; look deep within and you will see.

*Your tapestry is forever evolving, looking more and more
  like Me.*
*Your goal is to stain the lives of others with what I've done
  in you.*
*Mark them with our crushings, and your poured-forth
  testimony.*

Our lives are a process of crushing and shaping as God works
on removing the impurities from us. He is focused on our com-
pleteness, not our comfort. He cares greatly about the final work of
art. When we are in times of trouble, when we are feeling pressed
down, all the impurities flow to the top, and suddenly all we
thought we were, we are not, and we become awakened to our need
for God. "Now, O LORD, you are
our Father; we are the clay, and
you are our potter; we are all the
work of your hand" (Isaiah 64:8).
The potter molds the clay and
places the ugly gray rough piece
into a 900-degree oven, and later
miraculously removes a smooth, solid, yet delicate, piece of beautiful art, free of all impurities, ready to bring pleasure to its maker.
Our potter is our God. He is interested in our purified love for
Him and more interested in our walk than in our works.

> *The God-crazy
> journey is lived with
> a limitless God.*

What does it mean to stain the lives of others with our crushings? We must first begin with some God-crazy everyday living
steps, and we must love ourselves. Why is the idea of loving ourselves so essential in the path to becoming God-crazy women? If
we cannot give grace to ourselves, if we cannot give ourselves the
love we deserve and see ourselves as God sees us, then how can we
fulfill the purpose He has for our lives? How can we love others? If
only we could have as much love, compassion, and forgiveness for
ourselves as we do for others, we would all be soaring high on this
life of wonder and joy.

As you learn the five steps in this chapter, you will understand how the view from on high changes your perspective and brings transformation to your life. May this be a new beginning for you as you step out in your journey to becoming a God-crazy woman. These steps also lead you to a higher ground. When we rise up out of ourselves and see the world and our potential and possibility, we have an opportunity to see life with God's eyes. The view from here is high above the ordinary. The view from here allows us to see beyond the lies and to the truth of what abundant living is.

> *It's all over now. The strange mistrust I had*
> *of myself, of my own being, has flown,*
> *I believe forever. That conflict is done. I am*
> *reconciled to myself, to the poor, poor,*
> *shell of me. How easy it is to hate oneself!*
> *True grace is in forgetting; yet if pride could*
> *die in us, the supreme grace would be to love*
> *oneself in all simplicity as one would love*
> *any member of the Body of Christ.*
> *Does it really matter? Grace is everywhere.*
>
> —GEORGES BERNANOS

Five Steps to Becoming a God-Crazy Woman

The five steps to go from winter to spring are: *embrace, speak, act, will,* and *become.* These can sound like positive self-talk, but these principles are so much more than upbeat words—they are essential steps to being effective for God. Thinking positively about life and who we are and actually applying godly principles to our lives helps us make the switch from being self-centered to being God-centered. Instead of sitting in a car that remains in the garage while you dream of life adventures, you actually hit the open road toward God's heart and your purpose.

Step One—Engage in the Embrace

*"So do not fear, for I am with you; do not be dismayed,
for I am your God. I will strengthen you and help you;
I will uphold you with my righteous right hand"
(Isaiah 41:10 NIV).*

As we learn to take hold of God's truths, we also get to rest in God's strong embrace and are held up by His righteousness. Imagine what it is like to crawl up in His lap and feel His arms enveloping you with strength, love, and security. What comfort and peace this image brings. It is so easy for us to forget how close God is to us. We view Him as far away, somewhere out there watching us. When we accept Christ, God embraces us with everything He has. When we surrender, we also give over all that we have, do, dream, say, and think to His embrace.

What happens when we are in the arms of someone we love? Everything else around us fades and the problems that occupied all of our thoughts and emotions don't seem as huge, as demanding. When we are engaged in His embrace, we are less inclined to hang on to the comments and judgments of others as though our value depended upon it.

The God-crazy journey is lived with a limitless God. He wants to give you all the desires of your heart. You don't even realize you desire some of the things He wants to fulfill in you. "Why would God want to do that for me?" some might ask. Why wouldn't He? He has embraced you, adopted you, and longs for a relationship with you. Return His embrace and receive from Him all He wants to do in your life.

This next story sounds like a movie, but it really happened. When my sister Chris was in her early twenties, she met a young boy who, in his birth country, was considered a prince. He was tall, dark, handsome, and very wealthy. My sister was smitten by him and he by her. They fell for one another (see…just like a movie) and for a while were caught up in their own world filled with happiness and the joys of new love. But it would not be long before the reality of the young man's responsibilities rose up and could no longer be ignored. He would have to choose between the love he had for my sister and the calling he had on his life. If he married Chris, he'd be humiliating his family by dishonoring them, and he'd be cut off from his family and his inheritance forever. Everything was awaiting him at home, and his family was putting pressure on him to return. As the months passed, he began to prepare to leave Chris and return to the calling he had on his life, his country, and his duty. As heartbreaking as the goodbye was, even Chris knew it was what had to be done. I guess if it were really a movie we would love, he would have ignored his royal calling and married my sister. They'd be poor, but happy…maybe. This was real life, and real life required that this boy answer his purpose and call over his desire.

Although this young man understood his earthly calling and embraced it, that didn't make it an easy choice. His inheritance of responsibility and family legacy was only temporary, yet it was greater than anything else in his life. Though he was young, he still understood the greater vision, the fact that his decisions would affect generations to come. What is standing in the way of you embracing God and the inheritance He has for you? Our inheritance is so much greater than that of any earthly kingdom. Do we see the greater vision? Are we willing to answer the calling and purpose on our life, not out of obligation, but out of our passionate love affair with God? Unlike this young man whose purpose was driven mainly out of duty, our purpose is driven out of our love for Christ. Is there something you want more than God Himself?

When you head toward God-crazy living, you don't do things for Him simply out of duty; instead, you develop a desire to please Him and to reach your God-given potential and purpose, even when that requires sacrifice. This journey we are now on will help us seek God's perspective before we move forward. I'm not just talking about the big job promotion or having another baby or purchasing a new home. We tend to involve God when we face big decisions. But God wants us to bring the small things to Him as well. Once you start doing this, it will feel so good and right to bring everything before your Creator. This isn't a lesson in gaining God's permission...it's a lesson in embracing our heavenly inheritance. It's only when we walk with God in the small things, and daily engage in our passionate pursuit of His love, that the purpose and destiny of our lives unfolds.

If you are married, then you know the importance of running decisions by your spouse. Well, God is our eternal husband, and we should bring everything to Him and filter everything through His Word. We should hold up what He loves and turn from what He abhors. We may fall down a few times, but we will want to rise up and keep going to honor the One who embraces us so tightly and who loves us unconditionally.

Step Two—Speak Truth

*"Avoid irreverent babble, for it will lead people into
more and more ungodliness, and their talk will spread
like gangrene" (2 Timothy 2:16-17).*

When we return the embrace and feel the value of being a child of God, we will speak to ourselves in a different way than we did when we had a distorted view of ourselves. When lies enter our thought life, we will recognize them and resist believing them because we understand our identity is in Christ. But even in the comfort of God's embrace, doubts of the past can sneak into our thinking. If we have a spirit of self-loathing, then everything we say to ourselves will be through a filter of negativity. We put ourselves down and never adopt the peace of mind and the tranquility of heart God intended us to have because we are conflicted within ourselves. This is right where the enemy would want to keep you. He wants to be able to distract you from hearing or seeing God's purpose and direction. Instead of treading on the path God is guiding you toward, you will want to follow this tangent or that side road. Your focus will be on yourself, your security, and what you think are godly motives when really they are just human insecurities born out of the enemy's prodding, prompting, and false promises.

Old patterns die hard. And often, even when we are changing, the people or patterns around us are not, so there are plenty of opportunities for lies or broken thinking to circle back to us. This is why it is so important to surround ourselves with truth and God's promises. If we distance ourselves from these pillars of strength, we are not able to grasp on to them when someone brings up a lie or presents a falsehood that looks so real that we are inclined to claim it as truth. A doubt might stir within us, but if we are not comparing the lie or the misjudgment to God's truth, then it can be easy to believe.

What we speak to ourselves is as important as what we speak to others. This can be tough for women to fully embrace. We say we believe it. We say we've heard that before and yes, we'll be better about it. Yet we can spend an entire morning berating ourselves for a mistake or slip of judgment and then spend an afternoon encouraging friends, bestowing compassion and grace on them for mistakes and eagerly passing along forgiveness for their transgressions big or small. We don't notice the huge gap between the lies we tell ourselves and the truths we will give to friends and strangers.

I spent many years with my thought life centered on me, and not in a nurturing way. This by itself is risky behavior. I was beating myself up constantly and had no mercy. I was buying into that distorted view of myself that I had used as a foundation in my life for so long. Once I received my freedom, I refused to be negative about myself and thought I had the problem licked. But I didn't. Have you been there? Unhealthy patterns can be hard to detect. But the evidence is there, and when our eyes are opened to truth we are often caught by surprise. "How did I not see that before?" In my life I finally looked around at my choices and my process for making choices and realized I had been putting no value—zilch— on my needs or desires; I only placed value on other people's needs. Now, this sounds Christian in theory. There is nothing wrong with putting others first. But when you only know how to do that, you lose yourself, you lose your sense of God's purpose for your life, and you forget to ask Him what *you* should be doing. You are no longer on that journey He designed for you. Sometimes women avoid turning their thoughts to their own spiritual health and growth because they don't want to know the truth. They are afraid of the emotions and the decisions that might arise when they do pay attention to their own heart. God wants you to care for others, but He also wants you whole and healthy and in a very active, engaged relationship with Him one-on-one.

For years I made decisions while standing on that shifting foundation of my feelings of worthlessness and shame. And these choices, made with false information, began to shape my life. It took me awhile to detect this behavior, and much longer to let it go. Freedom is something we have to fight for. It does not always come easy, and like the woman who had bled for many years and fought her way through the crowd to touch the edge of Jesus' robe in desperation to be healed (Matthew 9:20-22), we too must fight our way through to see our healing take place once and for all. We must be willing to let go of the lies in order to reach for the Healer and His truth. We must be willing to speak truth to our own heart so that the lies do not have a chance to take hold of us again.

It's funny how children will adopt our ways. If we are always speaking negatively of ourselves or others, our children will feel the freedom to do the same. I make it a point to listen to my daughter Madison as she shares with her friends both on the phone and in person. I make sure to remind her of our responsibility to what we say of others and the importance of not gossiping. One afternoon she came home, and I could tell she had been crying. She pulled me off by ourselves so we could discuss her day. "Mom, today was so emotional. All the girls in the class were crying." "Why?" I replied, concerned. "Our teacher asked all the girls (as a result of some backbiting rumors), to gather into a circle and ask forgiveness for things we said about each other and wrong attitudes we had toward one another."

The teacher's approach was one of great bravery. Initiating a peace treaty among 12 preteen girls was an amazing feat. I mean, who knew what the outcome would be? Great news! It was a peaceful ending. Madison went on to share how each of the girls had opened up and asked forgiveness for gossiping and plotting against each other. She shared with me how she had admitted to being jealous of one of the other girls and speaking about this girl in a mean way because of that envy. I was proud of my daughter for her openness in admitting her sin and her willingness to ask forgiveness, but what really excited me was the life lesson she was taught. Madison would always remember how when we are able to be honest and admit our shortcomings, the enemy is not able to have victory in our relationships. We all have moments where we speak against each other instead of for one another. Not only is it important that we speak godly promises and truths for ourselves, but for one another as well.

God-crazy women understand who they are in Christ, and they are so comfortable with this identity that they are able to speak oracles over others as God speaks oracles over them. Are you beginning to see yourself moving beyond your old self? Is the wind in your hair? Is a smile stretching across your face? I don't mean the polite smile you bring out for social occasions—I mean the grin that bubbles up out of your soul with absolute surprise and joy. Doesn't it feel good?

Step Three—When You Don't Feel It, Will It!

"Remind them to be submissive to rulers and authorities,
to be obedient, to be ready for every good work,
to speak evil of no one, to avoid quarreling, to be gentle,
and to show perfect courtesy toward all people" (Titus 3:1-2).

Our culture teaches us "If it doesn't feel good, don't do it. If it does feel good, it must be right." But the Christian life involves doing things we might not initially feel like doing. Remember the story about my sister's boyfriend? Making the right choice was not simple, and it was probably not even close to what felt right. When our human emotions are a part of a situation (and let's face it, when aren't they?), doing the right thing might be in opposition to those feelings.

When we know in our heart God is telling us to do something, we need to do it out of obedience and faithfulness. We obey because we trust in Him. And He often allows tough situations so that we can learn to trust Him in every area of our lives.

My mom was an extremely introverted person, even as a young adult. She was so shy that most people perceived her as a snob and didn't talk to her. It wasn't until God pressed her to step out of her shell that she overcame her anxiety. After she became a believer, the Lord began to reveal areas in her life that were deficient. One area in particular was in the area of relationships. Because of her shyness and insecurities, Mom could not reach out and connect with people. She also had grown to expect people to initiate connection because she was afraid to take the first step.

> *When God comes on the scene and becomes our director, we are transformed.*

God spoke to her heart and told her to reach out to others first rather than wait for them. It was not an easy command for her to follow, but it was a necessary one for her so that she could begin to share God's love with others. She often shares stories of how completely nervous she was in the beginning. And like most of us trying something new, there were probably moments when she wanted to run the other direction and beg God for a different assignment.

It took her many years to overcome the anxiety and stress associated with meeting new people and speaking in front of others, but eventually she did. When she learned to depend on God for the courage and when she surrendered to His will for her life, she was able to express her heart to others, and she could even sing and play guitar in front of complete strangers. These are all things God instructed her to do, and out of her obedience she has blessed the lives of thousands of people throughout the world as an evangelist.

Isn't it interesting that those things that feel completely against our nature can actually be the very actions God calls us to do? Have you experienced this? Maybe this book is your first step in obedience. Often we know which direction God is trying to lead us, but we resist it. Oh boy, do we fight it, right? Yet if we are prayerful, willing to embrace God and the forward journey of God-crazy surrender, and hear and speak truth in our lives, then our choices begin to align with God's purpose.

When God comes on the scene and becomes our director, we are transformed. We become new creatures with new capabilities. Who knows what road God will take us on if we will ourselves to be obedient? If we push beyond the little boxes we have created for ourselves, we will find a whole world awaiting us and a new life to be discovered. Do you put labels on yourself? Do you say such things as, "That's just not me," or "I'm not made like that"? Maybe you use spiritual language, such as "Why try that? It wouldn't be using my gifts," or "I'm not gifted in that." I'm all for women following their gifting because it is directly related to your purposed life; however, if we are acting out of fear and not out of submission, then we are back to the counterfeit faith and those fake claims on truth…in other words, *excuses*. What limits we put on ourselves when we say these things!

I have uncovered each of my gifts as a result of going down a road God asked me to travel. When the Israelites were being led to the Promised Land, it was far from what they had imagined. They began to question whether Moses was leading them in the right direction. They questioned whether they should have been set free from the very bondage they were in. If they would have been patient and obeyed God, they would have seen the Promised Land so much sooner. Sometimes the road to the Promised Land has deserts. It may even have some swamps, but if we follow and obey God and will ourselves to stay true to the journey, He will lead us to places far beyond our wildest dreams. And the discoveries along the way are worth it.

❀ GOD-CRAZY MOMENT ❀

When God asked me to do a magazine for women in 1999, I had no background in publishing, I had never used my writing for anything other than expressing my heart to family and friends, and I had no money or contacts. But I had God, and I knew from past experience that if He was in it, He would be the only contact I would need. The vision God had placed on my heart had ignited a passion in me that allowed me to will myself to His purpose. This passion gave me strength beyond my own limitations. It helped me persevere when I felt like giving up.

It was not always apparent to me that I was doing His will. Sometimes I just had His initial word to me to trust in. The God-crazy pursuit takes perseverance for us to finally reach the higher ground, the place of rich blessing. When I saw the movie *Amazing Grace,* I was so touched by the endurance and tremendous sacrifice William Wilberforce made in order to put an end to the slave trade. There was a moment where Wilberforce had just finished running a race with his best friend. Exhausted and gasping for air, his friend turns to Wilberforce and says, "Why is it when you stop running you feel the thorns?" How profound. Wilberforce had many thorns along the way, even his very life was at stake, but his passion and dedication to the greater vision was burning so deeply within his soul that he would have to renounce his very nature in order to quit.

There were many times I had to will myself to go on, will myself to believe for things greater than my circumstances. I knew that if I willed myself to the vision and continued to press on even when my feelings didn't coincide, God would bring me through, and I would see not only the birthing of the vision, but the completion of it. I knew if I could just keep on running the race, I would not feel the thorns that were coming at me, and the race would seem less difficult.

One night while up late, I broke down and began to cry. I did not feel I could go on another day, not even another minute. I lifted my head slightly and something caught my eye. It was a sticky note on the side of my computer. On it were the words "Never, never give up." *How did that get there?* I wondered. I looked a little closer and realized the handwriting was that of my then seven-year-old son, Joshua. I immediately ran to find Josh. I asked if he had written the words on the sticky note and placed it on my computer. "Yes, Mom," he answered quietly, as if he thought he was in trouble. "Why?" I asked. "Because, Mom, you can never, never give up the magazine."

We are now way beyond the place of labor with the magazine, and it has touched the lives of many women whose testimonies have inspired me. This in and of itself has been enough to make the journey well worth it. The road was hard, and it was a great labor, but the reward has been great. The greatest reward of all is what the journey has brought to my spiritual life. This far surpasses those difficulties and those late nights when I had to press on and avoid the doubts. I learned to will myself to obedience, to have faith in the midst of all hell breaking loose, and most important I have learned to embrace the Father in the same way He embraces me. Overcoming turns all those thorny, painful places into the sweet fruit of transformation in our lives, and therefore we are then able to help others to be transformed in their faith.

For the moment all discipline seems painful rather than pleasant, but later it yields the peaceful fruit of righteousness to those who have been trained by it.
HEBREWS 12:11

Step Four—Act Out Truth

*"Do not be deceived: God is not mocked, for whatever one sows,
that will he also reap. For the one who sows to his own flesh
will from the flesh reap corruption, but the one who sows to the
Spirit will from the Spirit reap eternal life" (Galatians 6:7-8).*

The highest heights will be reached when we begin to act out of
our spirit and resist our flesh. Our desire for God's best will flow
more naturally when we know who we are, who embraces us, and
who loves us unconditionally. When the seeds for a God-crazy life
are planted, the harvest will be actions that take us further and
deeper into God's purpose.

I have four wonderful kids, and sometimes they complain. One
of my sons (we won't mention names to protect the guilty) tends to
complain more than the others over the simplest tasks. The other
day I was completely blessed to find he had vacuumed the living
room, cleaned his room, and folded all his clothes in a shockingly
orderly fashion. Seriously, I was astounded. What was most impressive was that I had not asked him to do all he did. He did it out of
his love for me and his desire to please me, and his little face showed
how eager he was to display to me what he had accomplished. It
meant more to me than if I had instructed him to do it and he had
obeyed because it was an act of the heart. In our faith relationship
with God, it's important to act on the things He instructs us to do,
and it's even more important to make sure those acts are done out
of love and not duty. The fruit of acts done out of love is joy. Just
think of the pleasure it gives your Lord.

What is the state of your heart when you are doing things? Are
you rushing around with a huge to-do list that grows out of guilt
or the hope of keeping up appearances? As tiring as it is to function this way, it also becomes the easy way. We get in the mode of
autopilot and assume that because we are doing good, it's all part
of God's will for us and we are not supposed to stop and ask questions. Men might not be good at asking for directions when they are
driving and losing their way, but I think women often struggle to

stop and ask for help when they are maneuvering their way through life. We accept the idea that we are supposed to do it all, smile a lot, and keep up the good works and good appearances. But when we take a moment to be still before the Lord and fall to our knees, exhausted and empty, we can finally ask God for the help we need to live out His purpose rather than our to-do lists. It all comes out of relationship, not rules.

God-crazy joy comes with a rush when our eyes are opened to the adventure God has for us to live out. Yes, we will still get tired. Yes, we will still have responsibilities that feel either unimportant or so routine we barely notice them. But we will have the delight of serving God to the fullest. We will have passion for the direction of our heart and the path ahead of us. Our actions will mean something because they will come from this place of assurance in Christ. You've probably seen the bumper sticker that says "Practice random acts of kindness." Well, as much as I love that idea, practicing intentional acts of God's goodness and purpose is that much better, brighter, and bigger. You will feel the difference right away because when you give your time and energy and faithfulness and patience and talents to fulfill whatever it is God calls you to do, there will be the provision of God's peace. That feeling we get when we cross something off of our to-do list is nothing compared to the satisfaction of serving God and His calling in our lives with God-crazy commitment.

Step 5—Become God-Crazy Committed

"Commit your way to the LORD*; trust in him, and he will act.*
He will bring forth your righteousness as the light, the justice
of your cause like the noonday sun" (Psalm 37:5-6).

Eventually, if we embrace, speak, act, and will ourselves, we will become the God-crazy woman we were born to be. *Born to be.* This is so different from the world's call to become a version of someone else in order to receive success or admiration. God does not tell us to be like everybody else or to pursue acceptance by pretending to be someone we are not. God-crazy women are called to become themselves. We all find our identity in Christ—but we are all unique. You are so special to God. Only you are purposed for the things God has designed for you to do or say or be. But it all starts with our willingness to turn and embrace Him, to really understand His great love for you and me. This understanding of His unconditional love endears us to Him.

My son Jacob recently asked me if I loved him…if I really loved him. Love through the eyes of a nine-year-old boy goes something like this:

"Mama, if I didn't have arms, would you love me?"

"Yes, Jacob, I would love you."

"If my legs were chopped off, would you still love me?"

"Yes, Jacob, I would still love you."

"What if I didn't have any arms or legs, would you love me?"

"Oh, Jacob," I replied, "I will always love you no matter what. You cannot mess it up. There is nothing you could ever do that would change how much I love you."

One of my good friends says that to me all the time. "You can't mess it up, Borquez." When he says that to me, I really feel as if I cannot mess things up and that he will love me unconditionally no matter what.

I hope Jacob really knows I will always love him no matter what, but there is nothing I can do to make him believe. He has to receive it, just as we have to receive and believe that God's love for us is unconditional. You can't mess it up. He is going love you no matter what the situation. We may face the consequences of a mistake we make, but He will love us through it all. When you are disillusioned by your own imperfections, stumblings, and pain, remember the thief on the cross to whom Jesus turned and extended grace and love in the very last moments of his life. We can embrace, speak, act, and will ourselves all we want, but unless we really grasp the depth of which God loves us, we are not able to really be God crazy.

Once you commit to walk in all the other steps and have received and believed in God's love, you naturally *become* a God-crazy woman. You look beyond the limitations that used to confine you or keep you stuck in ruts of routine and fear-based patterns. But as desire and faith become purpose and passion, you will make significant progress in your journey. If you keep your focus on the Maker, the Potter, the God whom we embrace, you will not be discouraged by the winds of change that used to destroy your hopes. Becoming committed to this new life ushers you to God's heart time and time again.

The first steps are not always simple, but when they come from God and are mapped out just for you, a falter here or there will not keep you from your journey or your destination of the God-crazy life. In His will you'll experience security, deep nurturing, and unconditional love. You will have fun, you will surprise yourself with great strides and great heights, and you will discover one day that you are living that adventure you had only dreamed of in the past. For some of us, it's a dream beyond the dream we had for ourselves. And this shouldn't be a surprise (though it always is) because God's vision for us is so much more magnificent and inspiring and abundant than anything we could think of. All the more reason to trust His guidance, even if we are headed for a storm that shakes our human foundations and threatens our resolve. God is calling us to keep moving, keep flying, and keep listening for His unwavering call to become our best…His best.

This is so exciting because we have only just begun, and I can't imagine what God is going to show you during our time together as you follow the course He has laid out before you. My prayer is that He reveals to you the next step for your life, whether that next step is staying home with the kids, leading Sunday school, changing jobs, having a better attitude about the work you have now, getting an education, telling more people about Christ, visiting nursing homes, or something else. Whatever the jumping-off point might be, the journey for every believer is very different. So hang in there. Don't look at the world around you for validation of your direction;

look to God's face as you make that leap and feel for the first time the reason you were born with wings of faith and a heart of great beauty. You were meant to feel the wind of wonder on your face. You were meant for the God-crazy life.

❧ LA VIDA LOCA ❧

1. Do you see yourself in the arms of God? Or does He seem far away to you...off in the distance?

2. Do you desire to engage in the embrace? How will this change how you see God?

3. What are some truths in God's Word you can share with others regarding their circumstances or life issues?

4. Is your thought life encouraging to you? To others?

5. Have you spoken negative words over a sister in Christ? Have you asked her forgiveness? God's forgiveness?

6. When is the last time you did something for God you didn't feel like doing, but you did out of obedience?

7. Do you make excuses for things God would have you to do?

8. What are some things you would passionately enjoy doing for God out of love, not duty?

9. Are you beginning to see yourself fully on board for this great adventure? Are you on this road trip with me with the wind in your hair and your heart open to what God has planned?

10. Do you believe God is wanting to do something magnificent in your life?

❧ GOD-CRAZY PRAYER ❧

Lord, help me to engage in Your divine embrace so that I can see how close You are to me every day. Lord, let every word that comes out of my mouth, every thought that enters my mind, be good and pleasing to You. Hold every thought captive, and give me the ability to recognize when I am speaking negative words against myself or my sisters and brothers in Christ. Help me to remember to speak oracles of wisdom over others and over myself. Lord, give me ways to act out this abundance of love I feel for You. I long to show You my faithfulness by showing Your love to others. Bring me opportunities. Help me to will myself to obedience to You and to Your Word. Teach me to stop depending on my feelings so that I can depend only on You and Your truth. In Jesus' name. Amen.

5

JUMPING IN

Faith is the assurance of things hoped for,
the conviction of things not seen.

HEBREWS 11:1

The LORD *will guide* you continually and satisfy your desire in scorched places and make your bones strong; and you shall be like a watered garden, like a spring of water, whose waters do not fail" (Isaiah 58:11).

The scorched places of life, difficult trials, everyday stress, and challenges we often face leave us wanting relief. Some of us know where this relief is found, and others of us are running from the very thing that will revive us. Faith is something we all have a measure of (Romans 12:3 NASB). And it only takes a small amount to ignite the power of the Holy Spirit that helps us to overcome every obstacle. We cannot heed the leadings and the warnings of the Spirit without putting faith into practice.

During a time of worship at a retreat, I had my hands slightly lifted and turned up in praise. And in the Spirit, I saw a blaze of fire in the palm of my hands! (Whatever your beliefs are, please know that this was not an everyday thing for me, either. I am simply describing the experience as it happened to me.) I felt the Lord explain that this fire in my hands represented fire I had walked through, and that as a result of this overcoming I would be blessed. He spoke to my heart and said He would bless the work of my hands, and He was proud of me for pressing through the flames. At the time I was right in the midst of heartbreak, nothing in my life made any sense, and I certainly didn't *feel* I had passed all the tests God had brought my way. In fact, I felt as if I'd failed Him miserably at every turn. If the God-crazy adventure is all about the joy of the open road, I was smack-dab in the middle of a dead end.

When I shared about this experience, along with my feelings of uncertainty, to my mom years later, she did not hesitate before speaking some very key insights I will always remember. "Michelle, passing a test with perfection is never the goal. Getting back up over and over again in trials and overcoming when it feels as if you cannot go on, showing you believe when you don't understand, is the success of a believer." I needed to hear those words of wisdom from my mom to make sense of all that had taken place in my journey up to that point. I didn't question that the vision and message was of God, but I did start to feel unsure of His pleasure in my life and my decisions. How could the God of beauty and love be pleased with me now that I was standing in this human-made mess of life? But with this new understanding from my mother's heart for God, I could see that my unending love for God throughout the trials was a demonstration of my faith. Feelings do not equal faith. I had not done everything as perfectly as I would have liked, but I did not quit. Even when I felt like giving up, I pressed on. And *this* was pleasing to Him.

God-crazy faith occurs when our desire for Him is greater than our fear of taking the next step. We cannot expect ourselves to complete this journey with perfection, but by faith we will continue to walk in the desire to be perfected in Him in order to fulfill the purpose He has for us on this earth.

Experiencing the Shallow and Deep Places of Faith

I live in Tennessee where rivers are everywhere. Even in some of the suburban neighborhoods you will find rivers or creeks running through or along stretches of yard. During most weekends in the summer, you will find me near a body of water. I love gazing at the water's surface or dipping my toe in to watch the current flow around it. But I'm usually there on the edge. Jumping in seems to be for others. Carefree kids will yell "watch me" and release their hold on a rope attached to a tree limb and plummet into uncertain waters. I look at the mix of twigs and leaves rushing by and the

We must loosen our foothold on the earth before His love can carry us along.

reflection of the mud below and think how dirty the water seems. I, in my adult years, have become a bit particular, spoiled even…reluctant to become or appear dirty. But as the heat of the day wears on and sweat trickles down my back, I will eventually jump in. And wouldn't you know it, the act of completely throwing myself into the water is not only refreshing, it is an amazing relief.

This sensation in the physical world is similar to the delight we feel when we jump into the depths of the spiritual river of life—Christ Himself. The deeper we go, the more refreshed, the more relieved we will feel. In the physical life, I use the excuse of not wanting to get dirty to stay seated on the riverbank so poised and put together. In the spiritual life, I use the excuse of not wanting to appear stained or imperfect to stay firmly planted in one spot as God's rush of hope and cleansing forgiveness rushes by. But eventually I know what must happen. I am not fooling anyone by pretending to be something I am not. I am not fooling myself by saying I am satisfied or fine where I am when clearly I am miserable.

I jump, and I feel freedom.

And it is so refreshing.

Some of you may remember the Nestea commercial where they showed a person falling backward into a pool with a nice tall glass of iced tea, suggesting we all take the Nestea plunge. You just have to know this commercial sold a lot of tea for Nestea. Who doesn't want to experience the thrill of reckless abandonment? Who wouldn't want to take this plunge of delight? When we abandon ourselves and dive into the river, it is here where we are safe, free of all the troubles life holds. The plunge, the refreshing feeling of water in the heat of day, is only a relief because we are thirsty, we are desperate for the coolness and satisfaction. Are we desperate for God, and all the freedom and satisfaction He brings to us? He is our relief in times of trouble.

Ezekiel 47 has a great description of a river. Each stage of growth in our lives is presented by the different depths of the water described. Are we willing to go ankle-deep, knee-deep, waist-deep? Or are we ready to plunge into the water and swim? If you follow a river from beginning to end, you will discover that it takes on many different degrees of power as it travels throughout the land it conquers. In some places it's wide and forceful as water glides and explodes over the rocks. In other places it's calm as water gently caresses the barely disturbed riverbed. If you are standing on the shore, acting as an onlooker, I would challenge you to at least get in the water, for "without faith it is impossible to please God" (Hebrews 11:6).

Each of us has been given a measure of faith, and all of us are in a different place on the journey. Each step of faith is another step of growth in our lives, drawing us to depend even more fully on the One who made us and the journey we are to take.

So why would we want to be in the deep waters and embrace God-crazy faith? As long as we stand on the banks of the river of life and refuse to get in, we miss out on all God has in store for us. The farther out we go and the more we immerse ourselves in the river, the greater the blessings. We must loosen our foothold on the earth before His love can carry us along. While we look up at the sky and feel the coolness of His protection ushering us down the waterway, we can see for the first time the many other places He wants to take us. When we refuse to let Him manage our lives, we are saying no to the promises He has prepared for us. We miss this chance to see the scenery of a richer, more godly life.

Sometimes God allows the scorching sun to beat down on us or allows the water to swell and carry us farther than we wanted to go. Nevertheless, we only experience the river of life when we get in and let Him carry us. Some people are born with the desire to take to the river and to float freely under God's watch. They were born with a sense of this faith adventure and cannot wait to see which riverbank will be their next stop. Others might be spiritually alive and yet still be resistant to being immersed fully in God's will. They have to go through great difficulties and experience brokenness before they stumble to the water's edge and consider jumping in to receive healing and wholeness.

I imagine us on our road trip, talking to each other and to God, listening to good praise music, and watching the ever-changing view out of windows that have slight fingerprint smudges of chocolate, salt, and nacho flavoring from our road trip snack pile. One of us stretches, the other yawns, and we realize how road weary we are. God points, from the driver's seat, to our right, where we see shade trees, picnic benches, and a trailhead sign that says "River of Life—This Way" with an arrow.

Let's go to the river.

Testing the Waters

"Going on eastward with a measuring line in his hand,
the man measured a thousand cubits, and then led me
through the water, and it was ankle-deep. Again he
measured a thousand, and led me through the water,
and it was knee-deep" (Ezekiel 47:3-4).

If you have waded in only to the tops of your feet but are reluctant to dive in, don't be discouraged. Many of us remain in ankle-deep water until we have a deeper understanding of what the river offers. We like to be in control, we love to be able to come and go as we please, and most important we want to stay safe in the shallow water.

You dip your toes in just enough to barely touch the surface of the water, and slowly you move into the shallow places. You are completely able to move about with your feet on the river bottom while maintaining a sense of balance and safety. What you don't realize is the only safety we have is in Christ Himself. There are no guarantees in life, nothing that says we will be here another day or even another minute. In the trickling brook you can grab the earth's edge if you desire to get out. You can get so used to the mild current that there are very few surprises. Some of us stay in ankle-deep waters, letting God in, but not yet surrendering.

Experiencing the river in its fullness is not something we tend to think about. Some are completely satisfied experiencing the river in small doses. We will see heaven as believers even if we spend our whole lives standing in ankle-deep water, but we will not have an opportunity to see all the wonderful things God wants to do in our lives in order to expose His deep love for us while we're still here on this earth. So keep moving into the river, allowing the craziness of your faith to erupt rivers of living water in your soul.

In the knee-deep water of faith, the believer does not allow herself to be completely submerged, holding on just enough to the edge and to their own will to feel safe. We are good at creating our human limits so that we feel safe, aren't we? Unfortunately, we believe this *feeling* of safety and don't realize that we are actually taking a very big risk by staying close to the edge of our version of good living or security. Not many of us consider the limits we place on ourselves as risk because we have created them to *avoid* risk. But think of it this way: While we are clinging to limbs of financial security, or vines of fear and self-doubt, we are missing out on the miraculous things God can do once we jump in and let the water take us! Have you ever watched a friend blossom in the Lord's power for her life? If so, have you felt as though you were stuck knee-deep in mud while you waved to her as she rushed by on her way to His promises? Chances are, most of us have been there. We see how God can and does transform the lives of others, yet we hold on for dear life to our old life.

The ankle-deep waters and the knee-deep waters still leave us more or less in control of the outcome of our lives. God is someone we talk to when we are in trouble, and faith is something we activate mostly when we absolutely have no other choice but to believe. We may only be equipped to believe God for the things that come easily, still not believing for the impossible and still afraid to lose our bearings.

Are you so set in your ways that you are not able to trust God to do great things in your life?

God gave us His Word to build up the brethren, to equip the body in order to believe. Both the ankle-deep and the knee-deep faith are a part of our Christian journey, but it is essential for growth that we do not get stuck in shallow waters. We need to be always moving down the river to the deeper things of God.

Taking a Chance

"Again he measured a thousand, and led me through the water, and it was waist-deep" (Ezekiel 47:4).

There are those who find the small splash of waves across their knees boring or unsatisfying. We aren't quite ready to go jump into the rushing deep waters, so we find middle ground where we can still get across the river on our own, strategically planning each step we take. The water here is moving at a faster pace than in the quiet shallow places, but we can still maintain control and therefore God cannot completely use us to our fullest potential. These places in the river can be satisfying and are where many of us can live very easily for many years, if not most of our lives. Our view of more of the river and of a particular bend where the willows dip down and grace the water surface lead us to think we are far along the course of the river's life. The swirls of water about our waist give the appearance of movement, and we start to believe that we are indeed moving. What we don't realize is that beyond that bend there is still a long stretch of our purpose to be lived out with great joy and faith. What we don't want to admit is that the movement we experience is life rushing by us at great speed while we remain stagnant and unmovable.

Waist-deep faith is growth because we have learned to trust God for parts of lives, and we have tasted the sweetness of growth and communion. This is why it is difficult to realize the need to move even farther down the river. *Why move from this spot?* we think. Many of our friends are probably in this very spot. It feels good and there is a foundation of belief and deep love for the Lord. We can be used in mighty ways from here. Maybe we are finding our gifting at this point, and this seems to be the perfect place to stop and build a life while using that gifting for good. It's pleasant here. There are shade trees and the reassurance of birds singing from branches on high. A cool breeze reminds us of God's refreshing Spirit. We are certain that this is what the faith life is supposed to be. We have arrived. Why pull up the map of God's Word and see if we are meant to go any farther? Surely this is the place to remain.

Life feels normal and choices are based on an understanding of who God is and the power He has in our lives. But here in waist-deep water is exactly the place where we start to think God does change lives, but He is done changing our own. So we make choices grounded in biblical wisdom and from a God-loving heart, but we stop believing that He wants to transform us any further. In fact, we might even be hoping this is the case because we like it here; that is, until our choices or our difficulties and losses lead us to understand that we are intended to keep moving and to go beyond this comfortable spot. It's scary. I know it is. You might be at this very point in your life. If so, I pray that this is encouragement for you to shift your feet and allow God's strength to move in with the force of the waters from the Colorado River through the Hoover Dam. Hang on, don't resist, let go! You are heading to the place Ezekiel speaks of…the place where we are utterly reliant on God to carry us completely.

Fully Immersed

"Again he measured a thousand, and it was a river
I could not pass through, for the water had risen.
It was deep enough to swim in, a river that could
not be passed through" (Ezekiel 47:5).

A river that is wildly moving its way toward something cannot be stopped. Our feet can no longer help us maneuver along the slippery ground to the other side when the measures of water over land are great. Are your feet firmly planted to the point you cannot easily move where God wants to take you? Are you so set in your ways that you are not able to trust God to do great things in your life? Or are you able to believe God even when you do not know the outcome and when you cannot see what is up ahead?

You can let the river take you on the ride of your life, down into the deeper places where the water is rushing and wild. The adventure builds while moving down the river. It is inevitable that we will occasionally get stuck due to circumstances of our lives, trials, or even distractions, but getting back in the river is essential for growth in the area of faith We cannot pass through this river on our own, and we were not made to do so. God is the only one who can carry us through the force of waters that rage beyond our human strength. We might want our close friends or our spouse or even our children to be the ones to aid us, but when it is time, it is only God who is able. Do you see that as a gift yet? Or does that still strike fear in you?

The rest of our journey together will be related to this life of immersion. This is God-crazy faith and commitment from here on out. We will allow ourselves to recognize our fears and insecurities, but we won't reach for them. We will see them, feel them, and wave to them as we rush by on our way to a more passionate life of all-out faith and grace and deliverance. Faith draws us closer to God, just like trusting and believing in someone—whether it's a spouse or a friend—draws us closer together in relationship. The more we are able to trust someone, the deeper the relationship goes. The more we trust God, the more certain we become of His love and of our connection to Him and His purpose for us.

Our faith transforms us and keeps us from living in the destitute places where there is no growth. We need to allow our trials to lead us to the river instead of making us run the other way.

Shall We?

Should we do this? Is it time to jump in fully, completely, and deeply? We have been on the road awhile now. It would be refreshing, it would be a great relief, and it might even be just what we need to shift our focus from our old self to our new God-crazy life. I'm nervous, but I'm ready…are you? Read this following meditation, and when you are finished, close your eyes and try to imagine yourself by a river, slowly walking to the water's edge.

It's hot outside and the rays from the blistering sun are turned toward you. Parched from the heat of the day and desperate for the water to envelop you, you want nothing more than to partake of its refreshing coolness. You find a shallow place to step in, slowly moving one foot in front of the other until it reaches up over your ankles. The water is cool and invigorating as it splashes up against your legs, and you step in a little deeper.

You can hear the splashes and gurgles of the water as it moves its way along the carved-out path in the earth. You make your way downstream, and you can feel the water begin to rise up to your knees. The trickling brook, the peaceful water, is fast becoming a moving stream. You move with it as the water now begins to travel faster. Rising above your shoulders, the water splashes onto your face. Your feet are no longer able to touch the bottom, and what once sounded like a gentle whisper now sounds like a rushing wind. You are being lifted and carried by the rapid current, and the water swiftly gains speed as you become oblivious to the world around you.

Your focus remains steadfast and straight ahead as you wait patiently for the river to come to a halt and leave you resting in its waters. You see the end up ahead, excited for the ride to come to an end. Finally you land in the arms of the ocean tide, and it's here where the river meets the sea. It's here you are thrust into the depth of all the vast ocean offers, deep calling to deep. No more rushing water, no more rocky ground beneath you, just peaceful sea water quiet and tranquil. It's here where your journey ends. It's here where we meet God, where the river and the sea finally meet. Whether we slowly move into the trickling brook or jump into the deeper waters of the river, we are guided closer to intimacy with God, and finally into God's presence where we find serenity and peace.

❧ La Vida Loca ❦

1. Where are you in the river? The ankle-deep water, the knee-deep water, the waist-deep water, or are you moving fast down the rushing water of your faith?

2. What is keeping you from going to the next place in the water?

3. What have you held on to as your lifeline while wading into life?

4. How have you used excuses to keep you where you are?

5. Was there a time you tried to go deeper, but your fears overcame your faith?

6. Who do you know who has jumped in? How does their life inspire your own journey?

7. Do you keep others with you at the same depth of faith? Or is someone keeping you at the shallow place when you are ready for more?

8. When you were a kid and got in the water for the first time, were you quick to place your face in the cool blue?

Or did you hold back and wait for prodding? What do you think you need now as an adult to go deeper in faith and further along the journey?

9. Do you worry about what others will think if you dive in and get scared?

10. List the ways that God has held you up in the past. Let these acts of faithfulness encourage you forward in the river's depths.

❧ GOD-CRAZY PRAYER ❧

River of Life, I stand at Your water's edge and try to gather courage so that I can jump into Your mighty abundance. Lord, You know it isn't just fear that keeps me holding on to the trees, the earth, the people still firmly planted on the land—it's my lack of faith, my past, my concern about submitting my journey completely to You. Help me release my grip on the life I have had so that I can have the life You want for me. I'm ready. Show me how to jump! Don't let me be content with staying in the comfortable places, the safe places of the river, but instead move me down the river where the deeper places lie. In Jesus' name. Amen.

6

IMMERSED IN
GOD-CRAZY FAITH

*Surrender, total immersion in God's love,
feels strange or even scary. Our first experience with
freedom will be transforming.*

—MICHELLE BORQUEZ

So did you jump?

Are you fully immersed in God-crazy faith? If so, you know what it's like to feel your feet lift off the ground, to have your heart expand in your chest with both excitement and anticipation. You are in this for good, and God's powerful hands are guiding you from here on out. You can rest in this truth. He has already carried you over rocky terrain and dangerous spots where the overwhelming pressure of circumstances nearly pulled you under.

How does this version of faith differ from the faith we have been living out or the faith we see others invest their lives in? And if we have all been given some measure of faith, how are we to live out the faith we've been given? These are two questions I hope to answer for you in this chapter. The intimate relationship we hope to have with Christ begins with faith. It begins with living beyond what we see and living out what we know to be true in His Word.

Five Keys for Moving Toward or Staying in Deep Water

1. COMPREHEND THE SOURCE OF YOUR FAITH.

Jesus would say, "You of little faith" in situations where the people lacked vision and belief in the mission He was explaining. They could not comprehend His message even after they had seen with their eyes the miracles of God. Even if they were loyal in their own ways, they did not have the faith required to fully comprehend God's plan, His hope for them, and for those who came after. Even Jesus' disciples sometimes could not capture the greater vision Jesus was trying to communicate.

We are blessed that the Holy Spirit gives us insight and evidence to help us stay afloat in faith. This guidance is how we are able to see, hear, and believe. He is the living water in our lives. Out of relationship with Him we are able to draw our strength and believe, and it is only by the Spirit we are able to truly conceive of the things of the Spirit.

If we desire to fully embrace faith, we must be empowered by truth. God's Word is Truth. This verse is so essential to our faith: "Faith comes from hearing, and hearing through the word of Christ" (Romans 10:17).

2. BELIEVE IN THE VISION.

Have you ever been a part of a start-up company? What about a start-up church? It takes tremendous faith and resolve to do either of these things. First, you have a very small group of believers who are either with you or against you. The leader must communicate the vision to get the team passionate about accomplishing the goals. It takes tremendous focus and determination to really succeed. Each person is essential to the vision. Each person must wholeheartedly believe in the plan and their role in the plan so that they can endure the sacrifice and dedication it takes to turn vision into reality.

Jesus was sent by God to communicate the vision of His Father and to share with us the good news of all He had for us if we would follow Him. While the journey is not easy or without struggles, trials, disappointments—and even humiliation and failure—we can remain focused on what is ahead. We can stay clear in our thinking and committed in our resolve because we know God's banquet awaits us in the future. We know that we will share in that table's abundance, and we will have even greater, closer communion with the Lord at that time.

When we understand the vision Christ communicated to us in His Word and choose to walk with the understanding of the greater picture as opposed to living in the here and now, we are on our way. This doesn't mean that we write off anything and everything that is temporal because those elements of our lives are also of great importance: family, time with others, our work, our gifts, our hopes and dreams, our shelter, and our daily

Do you flow in and out of intentional living?

sustenance. Instead, we should give those very things over to God as offerings. God-crazy faith allows us the chance to see what God can do with these simple aspects of life. He turns mundane into miracles and ordinary into extraordinary.

Those who have a kingdom mentality keep their eyes on the vision. When a man came to Jesus and expressed his desire to go and bury his father, Jesus said to him, "Leave the dead to bury their dead" (Matthew 8:22). Jesus wasn't being insensitive about the man's loss or about his desire to honor customs; Jesus responded from the knowledge He had about the temporal state of our earthly bodies. The eternal matters of the kingdom outweighed the urgency to go and bury the dead. It was Jesus' way of communicating His greater purpose, the bigger plan He has, and His desire for us to rise above our earthly pursuits and enter into His living kingdom.

If we have Jesus Christ living in us, why then would we not want His purposes, His plan, and His heart on this earth to be fulfilled through us? This is what He meant when He said to be of the world but not in it. We have to live in the day-to-day, but the focus of our eyes must be on the world after this one. The one He has created for us. The one He spoke of when He said He is not of this world, but of the world to come (John 17:16). "If you were of the world, the world would love you as its own; but because you are not of the world, but I chose you out of the world, therefore the world hates you" (John 15:19).

Just as we focus on the river rushing toward the sea, we must also focus on this life's journey leading to the kingdom. We are here for a brief moment, and in this moment we must concentrate on what matters to God, even when it requires us to let go of our customs, our rituals, and our comforts. Jesus communicated this vision time and time again. He wanted those around Him and those of us now to hear those words and to be emboldened to stand in our role and purpose.

3. LIVE INTENTIONALLY.

Living intentionally helps us move within our role and purpose. Living intentionally requires us to look beyond what is seen and to believe in the unseen. Let's not get this confused with self-reliance...a sort of "I can make it happen through my actions" belief. Our reliance must always be on God. We don't place faith in the action itself, but in the belief that God will make possible that which seems impossible. Intentional faith produces the fruit spoken about in Ezekiel 47. It also washes clean the dead places, the marshes and swamps in our lives.

When we live intentionally in our faith, we will have the courage to believe in the unknown. Faith believes what God has said is truth. Fear doubts what God has said to be true.

What does this look like when it's lived out?

When we infuse our daily living with this faith, we will see big and small changes. Just think, if we truly believe all of what God's Word says to be true, then we can believe that He will give us strength, that there is healing, that we can forgive, that we can be restored, that we can witness peoples' lives transformed from darkness to light, that we can love our enemies, and so much more. Many promises fill the abundant life shaped by God-crazy faith.

Do you flow in and out of intentional living? It can be easy to have a wavering faith. It's not so easy to remain steadfast, but the rewards for remaining focused on God's plan for you are so very great. A way to remain strong in your purpose is to develop your prayer life. Start your day with prayer, make time during the day to have prayerful conversations with the Lord, pray over your friends and with them, pray for your family and for those you encounter, and bring your day to a close with prayers of gratitude and thanksgiving.

If we truly believe and do not doubt, then by the power of the Holy Spirit we are able to be intentional in our faith regardless of our feelings, and we can receive the blessings of such faithfulness. Our own strength can only take us so far. We must rely on God if we are to surpass the natural and move to the supernatural. It is easy to believe and trust in things we know are possible, but let's move into the impossible. The things we know we cannot attain or grasp on our own...let's believe they too can happen.

Even when we intentionally choose to trust God, we are not guaranteed instant results. Our part is simply to have faith that He has good things for us, wonderful things for us, and no matter what the outcome of our prayer and our path, we are to trust Him and rest in knowing He is God.

 Not by might, not by power, but by my Spirit, says the LORD of hosts. ZECHARIAH 4:6

4. RELEASE THE ANCHORS OF ANGER.

Love fosters a rich faith life. When we view others and ourselves through the crystal-clear glasses of godly love, we see the world differently. Love keeps us tethered to God's heart and helps us discern what is of our nature and what is of His.

I have a dear friend who daily strives to forgive his former spouse. She had an affair during the marriage, and after their divorce she married that other man. Every day my friend prays for his wife and asks God to give her the desires of her heart. Now, I don't know about you, but this in itself is a miracle of God and a step of faith on my friend's part. However, his heart motive here is so important. If he is doing it out of love, then God will heal his heart and restore to him all that has been lost, but if he is simply repeating words to do the right thing, then he will not reap the benefits of true forgiveness. He must truly forgive his former wife in his heart and not just recite words.

In our own strength forgiveness and genuine release of our motives may seem absolutely impossible, but through the workings of the Holy Spirit within us we are able to be set free from whatever holds us back. We can even overcome the anger we have toward those who have caused us pain. Allowing God's Word to penetrate our hearts and seeing this world as a dwelling place and not an ending point to our lives can really help us release the wounds along the way.

When you consider the heaviness of anger, pain, and guilt, you realize you cannot journey far along the river's path if you are holding on to it all. I've had times when I wondered why God was not doing more to help me move forward. I'd look up at the sky and cry out to Him, and I would pray fervently for the open door or the ease of worry and a nudge in the right direction. I thought I was so wise to recognize that I was stuck in a place that was not providing me a chance to grow in my faith and my God-crazy purpose. However, I was so busy looking up at God to tell Him how I felt that I forgot to look down at all I was carrying with me. When I finally saw the huge anchors that were not only in my arms but wrapped around my legs, my heart, and my thoughts, I understood why I could not venture forward. It wasn't about God's lack of power or willingness to bring me along. It was about my lack of letting go.

I had the faith knowledge that it was time to heal and move on,

In the depths of my pain I experienced God's pursuit of me.

but I hadn't paid attention to the state of my faith life and my heart. Until I said my goodbyes to the pain, anger, and guilt and whatever else weighed me down, I wasn't ready to see my life through God's love.

Are your feet dragging along the river's floor? Do you look at God beseechingly, all the while avoiding glancing down at what is keeping you bogged down where you are? Release those anchors and let love cover you.

5. PRACTICE REPENTANCE.

Repentance leads us to truth, and this in turn helps us escape the traps of the enemy, who has purposed them to do his will (2 Timothy 2:25-26). Lack of repentance leads us to a place where we are vulnerable to the enemy, and we can easily be deceived. No longer is our faith pointing us to the purposes of God. No longer are we focused on the vision God has for our lives. Now we are instruments being used to counter God's will for us.

We must daily cleanse ourselves from unrighteousness and rid ourselves of outward sins such as drunkenness, sexual promiscuity, gossip, and the inward sins of the heart, such as anger, unforgiveness, lust, jealousy, envy, and pride. Every day we must perform inventory on our heart and ask ourselves what will keep us from the things God has purposed us for. God is faithful to fulfill His purposes in us regardless of our shortcomings, but sin bears consequences, and those consequences can easily become distractions from the things God has for our lives. It isn't as if God is looking down and saying to Himself, "Oh, look at those sinful creatures. I can have nothing to do with them." It is the sin itself that consumes us so that guilt, shame, and despair become our friends as opposed to faith, hope, and love. God loves us and forgives us, but when despair and shame become our friends, we are no longer able to focus on the things of God.

We must remember that we are made a new creature in Him and we are a beautiful being, but the ongoing battle of the flesh versus the spirit still exists, and we must be aware if we are to keep the faith.

Keeping the Faith

Have you ever felt disappointed with God? Angry with Him? Paul shares with us this statement of truth: "The saying is trustworthy for: If we have died with him, we will also live with him; If we endure, we will also reign with him; if we deny him, he will deny us; if we are faithless, he remains faithful—for he cannot deny himself" (2 Timothy 2:11-13). I love this passage of Scripture because it clearly states that even when we are faithless, God remains faithful. There have been moments in my life when I have felt faithless. When we go through difficult times, we might question how God could allow them to happen. We pray, we have faith, and yet the outcome isn't what we expect. People make choices, and God also decides ultimately what is best for our lives. There are things we won't understand, and yet our choice to trust Him regardless of the outcome is the way to please Him. Trusting Him when things don't make sense is the most difficult faith of all. Yet we set our mind and heart toward heaven, and we position ourselves to believe no matter what, and even when the results don't come, we press in and still believe.

I have had plenty of what I call "Job" experiences when my faith was greatly tested. In these places of despair I would face the choice to believe or not to believe. In the depths of my pain I experienced God's pursuit of me, and this pursuit caused me to realize His great love for me. This is where our hope lies: in God's relentless pursuit of us. When I have been lost or have lost my sense of direction and calling, He has found me. He pursued me and let me know He loves me. I'm not sure of the day or time it happened, but there was a point when I realized for the first time in my life that God truly loved me. Me…little ol' undeserving me! He cares when one of His sheep has wandered away from the fold. He cares when one of us is hurting, struggling with sin, or lost and alone. He pursues us and He loves us. What has been broken must be rebuilt. This can only be done if we allow God to come into the deep places in our soul and fill them with His love for us. His gift to us is His restoration and healing.

My Christian journey is one I have had to walk with God and God alone. We all do. The journey, even when it involves so many other people of importance, is still about you and God traveling together. This is hard sometimes, isn't it? We want other people in our lives to get us and make us better or make our way right and meaningful. But it is only God who can understand every part of our soul and who can lead us from our place of doubt or pain to a place of awareness and love. I'm in awe of how much Jesus loves me, and for the first time in my Christian walk I finally get it. He really does love me!

Do you doubt God's love on any level? Jumping into the depths of His care will wash away those lingering doubts. Are there moments when a cloud of circumstance covers your hope and you are not sure if there is anyone walking with you through the darkness? God-crazy faith is all about resting in the security of Jesus' love for you so that you can shine with His purpose, His radiance, and His wonder as you pursue life fully. God wants to commune with you every day, and most important, He knows you and accepts you as you are and *still* wants to be the One beside you through it all.

God-crazy women don't care if it looks…well, crazy to take a leap of faith and end up drenched. Let those who want to stay friends with their doubt remain on the sidelines. They can laugh. They can say you are mad to trust in a God you cannot see. They might even try to offer you a substitution for real faith. But once you swim back up to the water's surface, and you emerge glistening, new, whole, and ready for real faith adventure, those same naysayers will want to know your inner beauty secrets.

We can have complete freedom even in the midst of the darkest trials and abundant joy even in the worst of circumstances when we have faith—authentic, immersed, joyous, deep, unconditional faith.

It takes faith that sees beyond what is possible and focuses on the impossible.

What could be crazier?

❧ LA VIDA LOCA ❧

1. What are some God-crazy moments of faith in your life?

2. If God doesn't seem to answer your prayers, are you still able to believe? Why or why not?

3. What has been your source of faith? Do you turn to God's Word for your foundation?

4. Can you embrace Jesus' vision? Has it become real in your life?

5. What are some things you could give to God as an offering?

6. Which pieces of your life do you hold on to because you like the control?

7. What would living intentionally look like in your life?

8. Has repentance been a part of your faith? What do you want to bring before the Lord?

9. Do you trust God to turn your challenges and sins into His purposes?

10. When have you tasted the God-crazy life? When you first became a believer? Later? Still waiting?

❧ GOD-CRAZY PRAYER ❧

Lord, help me to keep the faith even in times of darkness, when all around me is cloudy and dim. Help me to see the truth when things seem impossible. By the power of the Holy Spirit, help me attain the impossible. Lord, keep my heart pure before You so I can have the faith needed to live out this life. Lord, help me to not lean on my strength and my knowledge, but on Your strength and Your wisdom. Lord, help me to not become distracted by the everyday things of this world, but help me see the greater vision and purpose, and empower me to do Your will, not the works of the enemy. Lord, when things don't make sense, when You do not do the things I am having faith to believe, help my faith to remain steadfast in You and not in faith itself. Please forgive me for any sin that lies within my heart, help me to resist the enemy and sin itself, and cleanse me with living water. In Jesus' name. Amen.

O fragile little butterfly
So precious in My sight
With patience I designed you
And I long to see your flight

I've watched you grow and held you
So secure in My embrace
Now as you go into the wind
My heart aches for all you'll face

No longer will you feel
The warmth of My cocoon
But all that I possess
Now dwells inside of you

When wind and storms may find you
Take shelter in My wings
For Mine will not be broken
They are mighty in their strength

Never will I leave you
Wherever you may be
My Spirit will go with you
Over mountains, through the seas

Soar high, My little butterfly
Your wings of faith renewed
Fix your heart on heaven
For I have My eyes on you

—Michelle

7

HEALING THE
DEEP PLACES

*God's love fills those hurt places we have been hiding from
others and ourselves. It transforms us, inside and out.*

—MICHELLE BORQUEZ

When we understand that God is with us every step of the way
along our spiritual path, it gives us the security we need to journey
toward the deep places of the heart. Sometimes it's a place we have
ignored for years because it was inconvenient to bring up old wounds,
especially those buried under denial or efforts to forget. Sometimes
we are not even aware of the hurts our heart might harbor. This is
not about dredging up things you've given over to God. This is a
chance to recognize what might keep us from the freedom we need
to embrace the God-crazy adventure.

We live inside ourselves, and only God sees all we hold captive
there. Within our hearts is where transformation begins because
this is where our intimacy with Christ dwells. This transformation
within our hearts must take place before the transformation of our
lives can take place. We discover deep nooks and crannies where
we've hidden pain, shame, guilt, humiliation, family secrets, and
tragedy from others. All this time we thought we were hiding these

9

9

things from ourselves and God. This isn't an easy thing to do, but these secret places with their hidden pains need to be cleaned out.

We didn't do this at the beginning of our trip together because that would have been too soon. As hard as this is, let's do it while in fellowship. This journey has bonded us, and God is leading the way. So release the fear and grab His hand and head on. Chances are there are cobwebs from years of neglect. There is little light here, so come prepared with the light of Scripture and faith. God is ready and waiting, so don't be afraid to make this trek to the unknown location of your hurts.

You might have to return here a few times or even daily for a while to keep releasing your lingering worries and concerns to God. Not because He doesn't take them at our first offering, but because we can be slow learners when it comes to giving up our deepest wounds. Our hurts might be tied to behaviors we are still very involved in or at least around, so the past often brings to surface the struggles of our present. Be prepared for this. The healing of old wounds will impact your life today. It is almost as though this part of our adventure is time travel. First we go to the past, from far distant to maybe even more recent (there are always levels once we start digging), and as we give our findings to God and He works on them and we do the labor of letting them go, we also change how we will react to our current life challenges. So when we return to the present and claim hope for the future, it's with a greater understanding of who we are, God's healing power, and the woman we were always meant to be.

Once our hurts are in Jesus' hands, He will mold them and mold us so we can become all He desires us to be. We are made new by ordering the world within, aligning ourselves with the truths of His Word, and uncovering the thorns we have hidden from God and others. Often we have hidden information, issues, or flaws from ourselves, but there is no way to do that and keep on the path of authentic faith. And believe me, you don't want to miss out on a full, living, thriving relationship with Christ.

Heart Bruises

I will never forget my first date. Not because it was an absolutely celebrated evening. Quite the opposite is true. I was a naive 16-year-old who was about to become aware of the unfairness the world can offer at times. As I prepared for my date I did what any teen girl does. I dreamed of the evening's promise. Jesse was about 5'11" with dark hair and a smile that made me melt. He had the deepest chocolate-brown eyes and eyelashes so long and thick they perfectly lined the top of his eyelids.

It was the first dance of the year. I was new to high school and had come in as a sophomore instead of a freshman. I knew no one, but at the first football game of the year Jesse had spotted me out of the crowd and approached me with his pretty boy eyes and sparkling smile to ask me for a date. I responded with a quiet but unhesitant yes. I knew nothing about boys. I'd been a tomboy for most of my life, but over the summer I had blossomed. I looked more feminine and less like a boy than

That night...was suddenly my worst nightmare and the beginning of a life filled with shame and guilt.

I had the year before. When I was registering for the new school year, the boys would look my way, and it was exciting to be noticed but also a bit confusing. I was very unsure of myself, and boys were difficult for me to read, to understand, to be myself with. The thought of striking up a conversation with a boy seemed so beyond my capabilities. But I was flattered to be asked out on my first date ever.

Jesse picked me up right on time. I had changed my clothes, changed my hair, and changed my jewelry at least three times before I felt satisfied with the way I looked. Everything had to be perfect for this first date. I was such a romantic then (I still am), and like most girls, I'd read and heard stories of sweet first dates and the budding of true love. As I climbed into his big Ford truck I felt so grown up. I smiled and nervously smoothed my outfit and waited for the romantic date to begin. But before we could exchange much more than a hello, Jesse told me he had to stop at a convenience store. I waited for him to return, and when he came back and tossed a bag with some orange juice and a bottle of clear liquid next to me. I was still oblivious to anything he had planned. My mind was on the dance and how nerve-wracking but exciting it would be. I just hoped I could muster the courage to say more than "hello."

"One more stop," he said casually.

We pulled around behind the back of the school where he stopped the car. He reached into the grocery bag and removed the bottles. He poured out half of the orange juice from each of those bottles and then replaced the fluid with the clear liquid, which turned out to be vodka. He told me to down it so we could get to the dance. Wanting to be cool, I drank down the mixture with no problem. Not in the first few minutes anyway. But by the time we walked in to the area where the dance was underway, I could hardly stand. I'd lost all feeling in my little body and was completely out of control. I vaguely remember Jesse telling his best friend Rob and Rob's girlfriend Laurie that he needed to get me out of there before he got in trouble. Laurie volunteered her house since her parents were not around. The three friends managed to get me to the car and to Laurie's house, where Laurie took care of me while I got sick over and over again. She led me to her room and helped me lie down, and then she went out and shut the door.

I was in a daze, but after a few minutes I could hear Laurie telling Jesse to leave me alone. He ignored her pleading and came into the room. I looked up, so groggy and sick, and he was towering over my body and breathing heavily. Then he began forcing himself on me. I tried with all my might to resist him, but the alcohol had weakened me and his strength was much greater than mine. I couldn't get him off of me. That night, the night that should have been about fun, dancing, holding hands, and dreaming dreams, was suddenly my worst nightmare and the beginning of a life filled with shame and guilt. My innocence was gone and so was my trust.

It would be years later after getting saved that God would begin to heal the heart bruise I had received as a result of what happened with Jesse. Twenty-four years after the incident, Jesse gave me a formal apology, a complete miracle. With amazement I heard Jesse plead, "Michelle, please, please, forgive me for raping you." You'd think I would have welcomed his words with great anticipation, but I had forgiven him long before the words were spoken. This act of forgiveness was more beneficial for him at that point than for me. However, it was an amazing God-thing to hear the words "Will you forgive me?" from the one who'd caused me so much pain for many years.

The violent loss of my innocence would not be the last time I would face significant pain and trials in my life. Other bumps and bruises would be mine to bear. Innocence can be taken from us in many ways. Betrayals, disappointments, and violations can take many different forms. Most of us have walked through these fires, and some of us may or may not have moved on. I have tried to be careful to not allow my heart to become hardened. There are times I have started to put up layers of brick and mortar to keep people away from these places. Have you done this? Maybe you have even accomplished building a great wall by now. When we put layers up around our heart, when we harden ourselves so no one can get in, we also create the walls of our own prison. We become so shut up and shut down that we are not able to be vulnerable with others and a real and vulnerable relationship with Christ becomes more and more difficult.

But God's faithfulness finds a way through. He saves us from completing those walls and from reinforcing them over the years with more distance, bitterness, self-sufficiency, and fear. We might think we are using the best and strongest materials when building the protective fortress around our wounds, but God's grace and mercy flows right on through.

I know many of you have experienced deep pain, and you may even be thinking to yourself, *Michelle, what you went through was nothing compared to what I faced.* I have met people whose stories are so hard to hear it's difficult to believe they have survived to tell them. I have met others who have not had to endure the more serious trials of life, but we've all experienced difficulties, we've all been wronged at some point in time, and we've all had times when we can only fall to our knees and cry out to God for help. The decision to choose a road of forgiveness and love over a road of anger and hate turns burden to blessings in the course of the believer's life.

Choosing God's Heart

No matter what your situation is, Jesus wants you to lay your burdens on Him. Through this experience of grace and comfort, He calls us to love, to have mercy, to have compassion, to take up His cross and follow Him, to die to our own desires, and to serve those around us. When our hearts are hardened, we are unable to be His hands and express His love to those who need love—ourselves included. When our spirits are refreshed and we immerse ourselves fully in God's peace, we are able to be His feet and go wherever He wants us to go. We can be His eyes to see what we need to see, such as hurting people around us or even our own deep wounds. We have His heart to love those who seem unworthy, those who are the lowly, the unwanted.

Does this ability to love like this seem an impossible feat? For you and me on our own it isn't feasible, but when we ask God to give His heart of forgiveness to us, the capacity of our heart expands. The muscles of forgiveness and compassion bulk up. With this new strength, we are then asked to give forgiveness and to release the past. I've been amazed by how many women live in and function out of shame, guilt, and disappointment. There are many of us who have had hardships or who have never felt we measure up to the standards set by God, our parents, our spouses, the culture, our childhood dreams. But we are wrong in this thinking. We do measure up. We can find healing in Christ, and in this healing we will uncover our great worth in the eyes of the Lord. There is no other measure to reach. There is no other expectation to meet. If we can accept that God accepts us, we can embrace the beautiful joy of the God-crazy life.

Choosing to have God's heart is an everyday decision. If we don't pursue God's heart, we choose to let circumstances rule over us, and we lean toward unforgiveness rather than accepting a new perspective. But if we intentionally choose God's heart daily, we can be forgiving and change the circumstances rather than our hearts. This does not mean we walk around with a fake smile on our face. We will have times when hurt rules over us, sorrow consumes us, and unforgiveness is our friend, but it is in those times that we can rest in God's strength. When we confess our weakness to Him, we can receive His help to overcome every bruise, heartbreak, and wound.

We are programmed to believe that we make all of our choices from our heads. But the important choices are made in the heart. Every morning I have to choose Him over myself, over my desire to stay in my own space and harbor hatred, jealousy, unforgiveness, and self-pity. We create our own little worlds so

What is keeping us from allowing God to pour Himself into us?

that we can have a safe place. Creating a forbidden place where hidden sin or pain resides easily turns into a place of loneliness and isolation. Our efforts toward self-protection lead to a bitter heart rather than a God-crazy heart. The price of this protection is that we also cut ourselves off from others, including other believers and those God might have in our lives to help us with godly counsel. When we are left to our own wisdom, we tend to lose sight of the path and of our purpose. Purpose, we consider, is only for those who are whole and healed, so we rarely strive for our own sense of purpose. But even in our brokenness, God has a purpose planned for your life. This, my dear friend, is why it's so important to seek the healing and strength He offers. You will want this purpose to become your reality. You will want what is in store for you.

God sees and knows our hearts; there is nothing hidden from Him. We were made for relationship, and a God-crazy relationship begins with an open heart. Even though this goes against the human idea of success, we can be certain that as believers it's when we have a broken and contrite spirit that we are most open to possibility and purpose.

Broken and Whole

Why do we need to be broken to become strong in the Lord? Why does it often take us reaching that most shattered point in our lives to know God's grace in a way that inspires our God-crazy life? It doesn't seem fair, does it? Shouldn't living in faith and goodness be enough? Certainly that is pleasing to God. But I believe that when we are broken, we no longer have anything to lose. In this state of dependence on God for anything and everything, we discover what we should have or could have known all along—we are loved and He is the Healer. Everything is in pieces, and only God can mend us back together. We've learned to trust Him, to depend on Him, to allow Him to mold us and to deliver us.

What no eye has seen, nor ear heard,
nor the heart of man imagined, what God
has prepared for those who love him.
1 CORINTHIANS 2:9

Friend, there is deep joy in knowing all things work together for good for those who love God. There is joy in knowing that somehow, someway there is purpose and meaning even when we face the darkest valleys. I've said many times "I don't understand. Why me, Lord? Why have I had to endure such trials, such pain?" Why did God come to this earth only to be humiliated, betrayed, spit on, disappointed, thrown away, and ultimately murdered? Do we want to follow Jesus? Is this the road we must travel to do so? Are we willing to be humiliated, to fail, to be betrayed? If we thought about this for a millisecond, we would say no, wouldn't we? And yet to give up our lives for Christ is what we must do if we are really to fulfill His purposes for us and to reap abundant, submitted life. This very act of surrender leads us to the wonder of meaningful living.

Remember, what good is it if we gain the whole world yet forfeit our souls? (Mark 8:36). I say forfeiting our souls is the only way we will gain the whole world…God's world. This is the message of Christ. This is the cross and the resurrection. Jesus gave up everything He had and desired. He forfeited His own life, pride, and maybe even His desire to live a normal life like the rest of us because He was able to see the bigger picture, the greater plan, the higher ways. Our life is short and limited and limiting. We work so hard to protect the very thing God is asking us to give…our heart! It often takes change and times of hardship for us to wake up to this truth.

So why do we spend our whole lives building walls around our hearts? Is it to protect ourselves? From what, may I ask? If God be with us, who can be against us? If we close up our heart, the enemy has won the battle. We can no longer feel hurt or pain, but we can also no longer hear God when He speaks to us, or love others when they are crying out for love, or even receive love when someone wants to love us.

How do we obtain a heart of openness? How do we tear down the walls we have so carefully built up? It is amazing how quickly God can tear down what we have spent our whole lives building. We meticulously crafted each little brick we placed around our hearts, and in one moment God can allow something to come into our lives that crumbles the very foundation of our lies.

Jesus sternly addresses the Pharisees and points out their hearts before the disciples. "Woe to you, teachers of the law and Pharisees, you hypocrites! You are like whitewashed tombs, which look beautiful on the outside but on the inside are full of dead men's bones and everything unclean" (Matthew 23:27 NIV).

Jesus understood that the Pharisees did not have an open heart to hear, to receive, to change, to give, or to love. They were so concerned with the rules, regulations, and religious traditions of man that they were not able to recognize the King of kings. What is keeping us from allowing God to pour Himself into us? What rules, regulations, or religious traditions keep us distant not only from God, but from those He calls us to know or help or pray for? Do you fend off the very people who are intended to speak into your life in a way that is practical, spiritual, or personal? A heart of openness leads to relationships with others because people feel free to come to you with genuine concerns about their life or yours.

Ready to Repent

Talking about sin isn't much fun—unless it's someone else's sin. Who wants to talk about the muck in our own lives, especially when we know it's what is clogging up our hearts? That's hardly date talk or Friday-night-out-with-girlfriends talk. Some of us feel as though we rarely get a chance to talk about ourselves as it is, so why would we want to introduce a downer topic like sin if we have a captive audience in a kind friend or mentor?

Yet sin needs to be out in the open. If we go about leading a religious life as opposed to the life of restoration, we deny our sins rather than seek revelation about them. We are like the Pharisees who look white and pure on the outside but who have much that is unclean in their spirit.

On the other hand, we certainly don't go around reporting to everyone, "By the way, can you believe I gossiped today? Can you believe I drank too much last night? Can you believe I slipped and watched some pornography the other day? And I lusted after a man I work with!" It is easier and tidier to pretend we have it all together. How, exactly, do we introduce the topic of sin without soliciting strange looks or laughter?

Let's see…what would you do if you had a clogged pipe in the bathroom? Would you go ahead and use it anyway, hoping it would unclog itself? Would you go around pretending it wasn't clogged so you didn't have to deal with it at all? This seems ridiculous, doesn't it? After all, we cannot live without a functioning bathroom for long. How much more important to unblock our hearts and make them functioning again.

My mom gave me a great way to explain to my kids why just a little bit of sin still contaminates the heart. She'd heard the analogy from a speaker and used the example to describe sin to my brothers when they were little (my sister and I were fortunate enough to not have seen the demonstration). Now before I go any further, I don't necessarily encourage this illustration, but it did impact my brothers, and it still makes me laugh. One day my mom made up this wonderful batch of brownies from scratch, and before she poured the rich batter into the pan, she asked my brothers to go and get some dog poop out in the yard so she could mix it in with the brownies. "Just a little, though, so it won't hurt the rest of the brownie mix," she added nonchalantly. My brothers were shocked and told Mom that even a little dog poop would ruin the brownies. Who would eat them with poop as an ingredient? "Well...of course you are right," she told them and continued, "it is the same with sin. A little bit of sin contaminates the heart in the same way a little bit of poop in some brownie mix would ruin the whole batch."

This is a little vivid and maybe not something you will hear preached from the pulpit, but the truth is there in the story of dog poop. And when we pretend that our life is perfectly fine and delightful without giving our heart to God for cleansing, then the smelly truth will eventually contaminate our land of pretend purity.

  Then desire when it is conceived gives birth to sin, and sin when it is fully grown brings forth death.
JAMES 1:14-15

Sin in our lives can go undetected for a long time. We might be in denial that an activity is sinful in nature. Or we are ignorant of what sin is. But no matter the reason for the neglect, the sin will ultimately clog up our heart and keep us from full communion with the Lord. It isn't the sin and it isn't God rejecting us that keeps us from relationship with Him; it's the consequences of sin that keep us from experiencing the intimate relationship we so desire with Christ. If we hide anything in our relationship with friends and family members, we feel the distance of this disconnection over time. It might start with little things—maybe we feel guilty being around them, so we make excuses to get together less often, or we stop confiding in them for other things because we have sacrificed the intimacy of full disclosure. They might begin to sense the distance and interpret it as rejection or anger when it has nothing to do with them and everything to do with us.

It is the same in our relationship with Christ. If we sin and do not confess it and relinquish it to God, then it provides us with false excuses to step further and further away from God's embrace. Talk about backward! This is exactly why surrender is at the very beginning of our God-crazy adventure. When we do not surrender our sin and our lives to Christ, we start heading in the wrong direction. When Adam and Eve sinned, they ran and hid from God. They were separated from Him not because He shunned them or threw them away, but because they were so ashamed they could not face Him.

A little sin, a little desire toward sinful behavior, can eventually bring forth a regular practice of sin and certain behaviors that distance us from pure love and purpose. When sin rises up in any form we have two choices, to walk away and sin no more, or to continue in it and deal with all the consequences of it—including our distance from God. There are three necessary steps to working through our sin. The three R's:

1. *Reveal the sin.* As soon as you see the sign of sin in your life, reveal it. Exposing sin in our lives to people who are deemed safe and trustworthy helps put an end to it.

2. *Take responsibility for your sin.* Don't try to find ways to justify it. When one of my sons admitted to doing something wrong and began to qualify his behavior, I told him that if he won't look at himself and accept responsibility for his sin, then he will only delay what God wants to do through the situation.

3. *Allow a time of restoration.* Ask God to heal your heart if there are wounds related to the sin. Pray for complete restoration from the sin itself.

A Moment of Weakness

We've established that the worst thing we can do with sin is hide it. And as easy as it is to say "Amen, sister!" it can be difficult to live out that rule of the heart. We want to bring along our sin and secret behaviors, and we kid ourselves by saying it won't be any trouble at all on our journey toward God crazy. You'll just tuck it away in a roller bag and lock it in the trunk? Nobody will know the difference, and we can still keep moving forward, right?

We've all been there. We've all stuffed a sin or two in the baggage of our life and tried to carry it along with us even as we are trying to get healthier and more Christlike. Do we ever really believe this works? I guess we do...at least up to a point, and that is usually a breaking point.

I was struggling with some sin in my life, and I knew I needed help to overcome it. Yet I didn't want to share it with anyone because who wants to share icky stuff when it is much more pleasant to talk about all the good things we do, say, or ponder? On the other hand, I knew if I didn't eventually share it and expose it to the light, then this occasional struggle could turn into a full-blown addiction. So I arranged to meet with a mentor and shared the "stuff" happening in my life.

What I loved so much about my friend's response was that she in no way condemned me (maybe she saw that I was doing plenty of that myself). Instead, she sat back, looked at me, and said, "So, you learned something?" "Yeah," I replied, "I learned something." It was that simple. She was calling me to learn from my situation and to move forward from it (not with that sin in tow, however). With the truth out in the open, there was no need to dwell on how bad it was or swing the other way and talk about how insignificant it was. She didn't dismiss it at all; rather, she called me into accountability to grow from it. By sharing with her, I was no longer trying to shove my sin into the trunk in the dark of night. It feels so good to be out from under the cover of sin. I was out in the open, so was my heart, and I could give it up to God completely to be free. I learned a great deal from that time with my friend. Now when I have sinned, I admit I have sinned. I don't try to find ways to rationalize away or trivialize it or repackage it into something prettier than it is.

If you deny the sin in your life, it will keep you from repentance. And if the enemy can keep you from repentance, he can keep you from freedom. Remember, legalistic religion hides truth and keeps us in denial because it is all based on our ability to look good on the outside. Restorative, God-crazy Christianity reveals truth, mends our flaws with love, delivers us from our sin, and restores our hearts.

❧ LA VIDA LOCA ❧

1. When do you most feel God's eyes on you? Do you believe He is watching over you?

2. What have you been holding inside that you need to bring before the Lord?

3. How have past heartaches kept you from God-crazy faith?

4. Do you believe that God heals the deepest wounds?

5. Are you a wall builder? List hurts or sins you are trying to hide behind that wall.

6. How has God already used your brokenness to lead you to deeper faith?

7. When was your last really good "Why me?" pity party? Are you still having it? What will release you from this focus on your pain?

8. Is your sin starting to smell? Who in your life can help you stay accountable to making a change?

9. Way back when we faced surrender and submission, did you mentally stuff the trunk with your sin to conveniently avoid dealing with it? Be honest.

10. How does God-crazy faith differ from the faith you have been embracing? Is your heart restored?

❀ GOD-CRAZY PRAYER ❀

Lord, I have carried some hurts with me for a long time and a long way. I have become used to the weight of them, the feel of the ache they cause me each time they surface. As I rely on the faith that comes from You, may I give these heart bruises to You each time I recognize them. I want them wholly in Your care and no longer in my possession. May I step beyond the false sense of security I have when I do everything on my own so that I can give all that I am and all that I am becoming to You. In Jesus' name. Amen.

8

THE ABUNDANCE OF
A WHOLE HEART

*If we are to accomplish our personal purpose
and passion in Christ, we must first realize that our inner
beauty is our greatest strength. We must believe that we
deserve and are made for wholeness. When we can see
ourselves as God sees us, we have an ally we can conquer
the world with, and that ally is ourselves.*

—MICHELLE BORQUEZ

You will recall that the God-crazy woman does five things: embraces, speaks, acts, wills, and becomes. These are more than a few items on a list of good behavior practices; these are stepping-stones to a God-crazy heart. We discussed these faith steps earlier, but now we will walk through them together in a way that will open up your heart to a richer, livelier, and more powerful journey.

When our heart is clear of the debris from our past pain and receptive to God's best, we are able to love *with* God's love and *without* our human limitations. Compassion pours from a pure place rather than a sense of obligation or fear of doing the wrong thing. Have you ever encountered someone who made you uncomfortable because of their great need? Sometimes their need reflects our own, and we are unable to work past our own wounds. Other times we see another's need as too great for us to fix. We like to fix other people, don't we? Let me correct that. We often like to offer up quick fixes for someone else's problem because the investment required to love them unconditionally through healing can be so overwhelming. And it will continue to be overwhelming as long as we depend on our abilities and tools rather than God's strength. We'll explore how a change in heart—an exchange of our heart for God's—will change how you see others, yourself, your relationship with the Lord, and your direction.

> *God-crazy faith grows in leaps and bounds when we cling to confidence in Christ alone.*

My parents definitely taught me how to love others and have a heart of openness to embrace those who I normally would not embrace. I grew up in Las Vegas, of all places. "Sin City," where prostitution and gambling are everywhere. "What happens in Vegas, stays in Vegas" is the slogan marketing professionals came up with to state the ugly truth: Vegas is a place to live a life without boundaries while you are visiting, and no one will say a thing.

When my dad preached, he often quoted this verse: "Where sin increased, grace abounded all the more" (Romans 5:20 NASB). This is so true in larger cities where dark is very dark and light is very obvious. Right in the middle of all those casinos, Christians were meeting and praising God! I think if Jesus came today we'd find Him in these kinds of places, talking to the people and asking them to follow Him.

When my parents came to know Christ, it was radical, at least compared to the North American church as we know it today. Looking back I can see we were living out the New Testament church. We had prayer meetings in our home that could last all day or all night. My parents would pray all hours of the night if one of us was sick or if a friend, neighbor, or stranger was sick. One of the most influential acts of servanthood my parents displayed would be to invite strangers, or what I would call "oddlings," to our house for a meal or to stay for a while. And these oddlings were people who were the most down and out—the broken, the depressed, the dirty, the lonely, the lost—and they all seemed to enter our home under a cloud of hopelessness. To society they would be considered odd, strange, and outcast.

I remember one woman in particular who smelled so horrible I could barely stand to be next to her. She looked as though she hadn't showered in months. Her name was Olivia, and she was an angry soul of a woman who carried herself like the broken vessel that she was. But my mother didn't mind that. She saw beyond the pain Olivia carried, beyond her unbathed body, beyond her burdens, and brought her over to the house frequently. In the years that would follow, Olivia would become a part of our family. Mom spent many, many hours with her on the phone, encouraging her and speaking the Word of God over her. My young eyes watched Olivia's transformation take place. Over the course of a few years, Olivia became a completely different person. My mom chose to have a relationship with Olivia, and because Mom earned her trust, she was able to offer her practical, emotional, physical, and spiritual guidance and assistance. As time went on, Olivia's heart changed and this led to outward transformation. She walked with courage and confidence. It was amazing to see how a heart change could lead to a countenance change. Olivia's face was brighter and smoother, and she was finally smiling. Reflecting back on the situation, I can only imagine the patience my mom needed to journey with Olivia, the eyes she needed to see beyond a devastated woman's flaws, and the hope she needed to believe in Olivia's possibilities.

She had God's heart for Olivia.

Mom and Dad lived out the gospel and taught us to live it out as well. They taught us to keep our hearts open to the people Christ calls us to love. Sharing my heart with others and opening my life to them keeps me alive in my Christianity. I strive to stay aware of encounters with other Olivias along my path, and I pray that I will have Christ's heart each time.

Embracing a Heart of Humility

Our culture might confuse humility with weakness, especially because humility is a characteristic not often found or nurtured in people. We are encouraged to be the best and do the best, and be proud of those accomplishments. There is nothing wrong with this when we act out of a heart of humility, but until we learn humility, it's hard to keep our egos in check.

False humility can be as much of a distraction from the things God has for you as anything else. I have met many women especially who have been taught to believe they are undeserving of credit or attention of any kind. They live their lives thinking they are lesser than everyone in such a way that they are crippled when God calls them forward in their faith and their faith journey. If we are always saying "I'm not able to do that," we are 1) relying on our ability and not on God's ability and 2) practicing a false sense of humility that turns us away from the opportunity to serve instead of turning us toward God's purpose for us.

If we call ourselves "nothing" and reinforce this everywhere we go, then we are not reflecting a mighty Lord and Savior. However, when we say "by God's strength I was able to do this task because my own strength was not enough," then we bring glory to God and our humility does not take away from what has been done in God and for Him. Embracing the challenges that He lays out before us is our way to humbly use the gifting He has imparted to each and every one of us. Arrogance comes from resting in our abilities. God-crazy faith grows in leaps and bounds when we cling to confidence in Christ alone.

I have met women who are always doing, going, helping, serving, and taking care of people and situations—even to the point of exhaustion. They express humility and obligation as they uphold this moral code of theirs, but in their hearts they are resentful and don't enjoy a moment of their service. Have you ever played the martyr in your life? I think we all have. I believe it's easy for Christians to fall into the trap of thinking that good works equal good faith. But what is going on inside us while we are jetting from the youth group to the school program to the church meeting to the charity function? Are we using our gifting and feeling energized by serving as God's hands? Or are we muttering under our breath how nobody else seems to want to help, nobody else steps up, and...here's a good one...nobody else can do it as well as we can.

Remember, God sees the heart. If we never speak up for ourselves, never walk in the authority God has given us, and only demonstrate our humility through physical expressions such as a quiet voice, timid smile, hunched shoulders, or a constant shrug because this is the mental picture we have of humility, we are forgetting that humility is born and resides in the heart. And only true humility honors God.

Jesus walked in authority from God. His focus was on the heavenly kingdom, not on exerting the world's version of power. While His response to people spitting on Him, insulting Him, and abusing Him could have been seen as weakness, it was the ultimate show of great power and humility. He knew His purpose and was passionate about truth. On the other hand, He was gentle in spirit and had love and compassion for those around Him. This same Jesus was not tolerant of those who were hurtful to others, or the Pharisees, who were made up of mainly self-righteous people. Jesus knew who He was. He understood His mission and His heart was pure. For us to adopt a spirit of humility, we must know who we are in Christ and be willing to walk in the power He has given us as heirs of the kingdom. We must know our mission and stay focused on the things He gives us to do. We must understand the impoverished state we are in without Christ so that we can embrace the power of the resurrection daily.

We might find it hard to believe that there are benefits to being poor. Something I find helpful to do is revisit author Monika

Hellwig's often-referenced list of advantages of being poor from her book *Good News for the Poor*. Read through it and let it settle into your heart and soul. It's eye-opening:

- The poor know they are in urgent need of being rescued.

- The poor know not only their dependence on God and on powerful people but also their interdependence on one another.

- The poor have no exaggerated sense of their own importance, and no exaggerated need of privacy.

- The poor expect little from competition and much from cooperation.

- The poor can distinguish between necessities and luxuries.

- The poor can wait, because they have acquired a kind of dogged patience.

- The fears of the poor are more realistic and less exaggerated because they already know that one can survive great suffering and want.

- When the poor have the saving word of Jesus preached to them, it sounds like good news and not like a threat or scolding.

It is essential that we understand our utter dependence on Christ, and that apart from Him we can do nothing. In the same way Hellwig shares about a poor person's mentality, we too must adapt the same mind-set when it comes to really understanding who we are without the love of Jesus in our lives, because without Him we are poor in spirit. Authentic humility rises out of this understanding and keeps us appreciative of all we have been given. Spoiled children who don't know the price paid for what they have are not pleasant to be around, nor are Christians who don't know the price that was paid for their freedom and the inheritance of the kingdom.

We must understand our impoverished state without Christ:

- We need to be rescued.
- We need each other.
- We need to open up our life and material things to others.
- We need to not exaggerate the importance of who we are (believe our own press).
- We need to cooperate, not compete.
- We need to care less about luxury and understand our needs are what God cares about.
- We need to be patient.
- We need to endure suffering.
- We need to embrace the Word of God like water to our soul.

If we have received great blessings in our lives, it doesn't mean we deserve to be treated like kings. Notice I didn't say queens, but kings. We walk around biting peoples heads off for not getting our drive-through order right or not cleaning our car perfectly at the car wash. Maybe we become agitated because someone takes too long in line. We go around ordering people, including our families, to do this or that, and we somehow justify it all by saying we deserve bigger and better and more for what we contribute in this life.

> *Understand that every word that falls from your lips has power.*

The feminist movement has taken pride in saying they brought "equal opportunity" to us as women. They were set and determined to legislate respect for women and to mark their line in the sand when it came to women getting what they deserve. Notice how the whole movement was built on what women didn't have and what they wanted. The strongest voices came out of a demanding position of entitlement. Christian women can adopt this same attitude rather easily without even realizing it, yet it is contrary to God's desire for women or men. When we focus on what we want, what we need, or what we think we have to have for us to be happy, we are unable to view the purposes God has for us. Our vision becomes so blurred and our heart becomes so cluttered that we cannot possibly expand our sense of giving and living. We become selfish instead of selfless.

So we must daily examine the motives of our hearts. Maybe even hourly, for that matter. Are you doing something for personal gain or recognition, or are you genuinely wanting to help someone in need or to move toward God's will for you? Are you satisfying a sense of guilt or satiating your hunger to follow God's leading? Our hope and prayer should be to adhere to the same humility Christ had, the same compassion He expressed, the same love He gave to others, and the same heart He had for every soul.

Speaking Truth in Love

"Death and life are in the power of the tongue, and those who love it will eat its fruit" (Proverbs 18:21). If our heart is filled with God's love, and we are humble of heart, then what comes out of our mouths should reflect that heart. This can be difficult for many of us. We often speak before we think, words sometimes tumble out when we should use discretion, and ultimately words can cause unintended pain when they could be used to inspire, encourage, heal, or unite.

If the tongue has the power to give life and the power to bring death, we need to be careful what we blurt out in haste or ignorance. A heart that is open and soft and generous will produce life-giving expressions. Can you imagine not having to monitor what you say because you speak only from a right and godly heart? It seems that it has become standard to tear others down for the sake of a humorous moment. Have you noticed that? We put others down under the guise of a joke, yet we often mean most of what we say.

My kids are the perfect example. Still learning how to express their opinions, they will rip into each other with verbal barbs. We will be riding along in the car and a quiet moment turns into tension. All it takes is one spark of sarcasm. This kind of talk between my four kids started to be so common that I prayed for a solution. I felt the Lord gave me wisdom when I decided to take a more biblical approach to the matter. Instead of spanking or grounding as punishment, I told the kids that if they say something ugly to another then they would have to wash the person's feet in addition to apologizing. This smelly prospect combined with the kids' pride was enough to motivate them to obey. I was thrilled to see the reaction the kids had to this new punishment. They thought I was a bit crazy for using such outdated methods, but in the long run it worked. It cleaned up their mouths, and over time they have gotten better and better about thinking before they speak.

How many times in the body of Christ have we wounded one another with an offhand remark? How many times have you been wounded by someone? Amazingly, many of us still feel the sting of hurtful words that were spoken to us as kids. Ladies, our tongues need to be controlled. We need to keep ourselves in check and respond to people when they approach us and not just react to them. Responding in love in a situation works every time. Embrace a new way of thinking and speaking. Understand that every word that falls from your lips has power...power to give life or power to give death. This perspective should help you to refrain from the gossip, the negative joking, the slanderous talk, and even the lies we can let slip so very easily from unguarded hearts and loose lips. "The good person out of the good treasure of his heart produces good, and the evil person out of his evil treasure produces evil, for out of the abundance of the heart his mouth speaks" (Luke 6:45).

Acts of Kindness

"If I speak in the tongues of men and of angels, but have not love, I am a noisy gong or clanging cymbal. And if I have prophetic powers, and understand all mysteries and all knowledge, and if I have all faith, so as to remove mountains, but have not love, I am nothing" (1 Corinthians 13:1). This verse is a powerful statement of truth. How many people can you think of that may walk in the power of God, ministering even with prophetic power and speaking in tongues of angels and of men, but are simply nothing without love? So what does this all mean? If we are going to do acts of kindness, they should be out of love. If we have a heart of openness and walk in humility, then our acts of kindness will be done out of love. Acts of kindness are simply the fruit of humility and our love for God.

A friend of mine who has always been a businessman one day felt the leading to pursue music. So he up and quit everything and moved to Nashville to be a musician. He has an immense heart and a love for both music and people that is very contagious. When he called and asked me to come hear him play a gig, I was eager to support his calling. Before I could say yes, he proceeded to tell me that he would be playing at a political fund-raiser. He knew that this was important information to include because I held different political views. He offered me an out, but I quickly assured him that I could support him.

When the evening approached, I wasn't apprehensive about attending. In fact, I was interested in hearing what other peoples' views were and what they planned to do in office. When I arrived people were friendly, and I found myself not only enjoying my friend's music, but also enjoying my conversations with some great people who had very different views from mine. And just as I was enjoying them, I sensed that they appreciated my openness to them. A few folks asked me to come on board and be a part of the campaign. I graciously declined, but this offer and the connection allowed me to talk to the candidate who was present about something much more important than politics…Jesus and a relationship with Him. This came out of a natural conversation regarding my background and beliefs. The people I met had a lot of questions, and a few of us agreed to meet again to discuss it all. My friend was surprised at how at ease I felt and was pleased I had come along to support him. We have different views, but instead of distancing myself from him, I did the opposite. I embraced him without conditions, and I learned in the process as well.

What good is it if we go and feed the poor,
tend to the sick, prophesy over people, heal the
brokenhearted, have faith to move mountains,
but have no love in our heart when we do so?

SEE 1 CORINTHIANS 13:1

I saw a bumper sticker that, I must admit, made me laugh the first time I read it, but then over time I began to think about what it really said: "The road to hell is paved with liberals." In reality the road to hell is paved with both liberals and conservatives according to 1 Corinthians 13:1, because I guarantee you that not all those conservatives are doing things in love. Bottom line, I am a Christian before I am anything else. When we show love through acts of kindness, it changes people forever. When you make this shift as a surrendered, immersed, God-crazy woman, you will see radical changes not only in our churches, but in our world around us. I also guarantee that we will experience wonderful changes in our own beliefs and views. Instead of expecting the worst in people, we begin to see the value and beauty of everyone. We cannot remain in a world of "us versus them" because God calls us to move beyond those distinctions if we are to ever understand faith in action. And God crazy is all about the faith in action, friend!

❀ GOD-CRAZY MOMENT ❀

My friend Peter is an extremely busy person; he's always on the go running his businesses. One time, he asked me to go with him to the hospital to visit a friend, Leslie, who has cancer. On the way, we stopped and picked up Popsicles for Leslie and her mom and sister. When we walked in, Leslie was thrilled to see us. You could tell she has such a love for my friend. He passed around the Popsicles and asked her about her week. I looked on as they all shared together.

Only 26 years old, Leslie went from a vibrant life full of promise to a life hanging by every positive word the doctor would bring her way and, of course, the hope for a miracle. I looked at the display of pictures hanging on the wall. They were all of Leslie and friends and family. She looked healthy and full of life in the photos. I said nothing as Peter talked with her as if everything were completely normal. It took every ounce of strength I had not to cry and just fall down on my knees before God, asking Him for reasons why such a young girl had to endure so much pain. I was so impressed with Peter's ability to easily share with this family he had not known well before. Leslie was an acquaintance, and Peter knew the family had no one in town to support them, so he wanted to serve them. *What a beautiful picture of Christ's love* was all I could think as we walked down the hospital halls and back to our cars. I learned a lot about kindness that day. I saw it as an intentional, spiritual, and committed act of faith and God's great love.

We are so busy in our lives that we assume focusing on ourselves is necessary for our survival. But when we intentionally go out of our way to do something for someone else, we experience something well beyond survival—authentic faith in action.

Become a Person Who Loves

The God-crazy adventure doesn't wait for the mood to shift or for circumstances to be perfect in order for us to give ourselves and our hearts with abandon. If God calls us to do something, we go for it. Sometimes we have to will ourselves to act first before things fall into place. Feelings may show up later as opposed to sooner, so don't let the way you feel dictate whether or not you give to others. Remember that God cares more about our growth than He does our comfort. Oh, boy. That's a hard one. Take a deep breath and think about those times of your greatest discomfort and hardship. More than likely they were also times of great growth. If you are going through such a time right now, I can offer you the encouragement of this truth: The pain, when given to God's faithful care, propels us toward greater strides in our adventure.

We have to be willing to open our hearts if we are going to represent Christ in a way He would want to be represented. Love is greater than sacrifice. Our Christian journey is always about taking steps that lead us deeper into that river of faith. As we jump off the edge, step further along the sloping ground beneath the rushing water, and ultimately are immersed in the deep, we will become our best God-crazy self. You may have heard the statement "True change does not occur until the pain of staying the same outweighs the pain of change." Submit yourself to His ways and ask the Lord to help you in taking steps toward a God-crazy life that is transformed and whole.

❧ La Vida Loca ❧

1. Become "others" oriented. A loving heart is one that gives without keeping track. Give from God's love. It is an endless source.

2. Embracing humility requires us to consider ourselves nothing and the work of Christ everything. In Christ we are given authority and power to do the things He

has called us to do. How have you embraced humility? What areas of your life need a bit of humility?

3. Look over the advantages of being poor. Which are the hardest for you to embrace in your current life? How does reading this list awaken you to new priorities?

4. Check your motives—are they godly? What is really behind all you do every day of your life? Are you caught up in the mind-set of a martyr?

5. Fight for freedom from past wounds. Freedom comes from a determination to press on and receive healing for things that have happened to us. Instead of Band-Aid solutions, here are some ways toward healing:

- Seek healing through counseling or prayer within your church.

- Ask God to show you where you need to forgive or seek forgiveness.

- Ask someone you feel safe with to help you pray for strength to overcome difficulties in your spiritual walk.

6. Speak love. Remember that every word out of our mouths speaks either life or death. Is gossip a part of your life? Recognize when you aren't speaking good things over people.

7. Act on your faith. Ask yourself this question: "Are there areas in my life I am giving with a pure heart? Do I think of ways to give to others of my gifting, my time, or my talent?"

8. Be willing. Is your heart willing to give? Would you say yes to God if He asked you to do something for someone else?

9. Become. Walk through these principles and become a woman who walks in the Spirit. What is your toughest

obstacle to a pure, God-crazy heart? Begin praying daily about this area.

10. What are your biggest concerns about letting go of your current lifestyle and way of faith in order to embrace the God-crazy life? Why do you think these concerns exist?

❧ GOD-CRAZY PRAYER ❧

Lord, open my heart. Heal the wounds of my past and begin to break away the mortar I have allowed to harden around my heart. Help me to get out and be Your hands, and help me to be open when others want to reach out to me. Lord, help me to forgive myself and others so I can be free enough to serve You and build relationship with those who love You. Help me meet and recognize the Olivias in my life so I can have an opportunity to give. Give me the strength to refrain from sin so that my heart will stay open to Your Word and Your purpose for my life. Forgive me of my sin today, and days past, and deliver me from the schemes of the evil one. Lord, help me not perform or do things out of duty, but give me a heart to love others. Give me a whole heart. In Jesus' name. Amen.

9

GOD'S PERFECT VISION

God chose the foolish things of the world to shame the
wise; God chose the weak things of the world to shame
the strong. He chose the lowly things of the world and
the despised things—and the things that are not—to
nullify the things that are, so that no one may boast before
him. It is because of him that you are in Christ Jesus,
who has become for us wisdom from God—that is, our
righteousness, holiness, and redemption. Therefore, as it is
written: "Let Him who boasts, boast in the Lord."

1 CORINTHIANS 1:27-31 NIV

You're ready for God-crazy living when you realize that somewhere
along the way you placed your hope in obligations and duties. You're
ready when the mere mention of "God crazy" stirs an internal
longing for a dynamic life of purpose instead of perfection.

It's time to move forward. Get back in the car with fresh ideas
and goals, and let's press on to more truths of the God-crazy life.
When the heart is open to God's possibility, we are ready for vision.
For this chapter, I define vision as the anticipation of and plan for
possible future events, dreams, and hopes. So what does God-crazy
vision look like? How do you get it? And then how can you move
toward it and in it?

The pursuit of godly vision requires a little patience and practice on our part. Most of us are by now quite used to ordering anything from furniture to groceries to medical supplies online. Before these goods make their way to our doorstep, we are able to see a picture of them on the computer screen from the comfort of our roller chair. Sometimes we can even read reviews to help us make a decision. This is the life. If we need something, we see it, we get detailed information, and we order it. But when we want spiritual, esoteric intangibles, what's a woman to do? Our on-demand lifestyle has us believing that all we have to do for fulfillment is plan our lives, make things happen, and create our own destiny. But if God-crazy vision is about anticipating our personal purpose and future in God's will, then it makes sense to seek our guidance from the only all-knowing, all-seeing source—God. We could guess how God will lead us and where He will lead us, but God *knows,* and He wants us to know our calling and our path by relying on His power.

Reaching for His Vision

When I look back on my life and the jobs I took as a result of obedience, I can see how God began to unfold His purpose in me years before I understood it. Early on in my Christian walk, I realized the importance of praying and seeking God's guidance for whatever assignment He had for me at the time. I knew I could trust Him to lead me to the perfect job for that time in life. I knew He would give me favor where favor was needed.

As a young teenager I dreamed of pursuing a career in modeling and acting, but the Lord had never opened that door while the longing was great. He waited until after I had accepted Him into my life before He brought those opportunities my way. By this time the longing had subsided and my heart became solely focused on ministry.

I came to know Christ at the age of 20. I was living in Scottsdale, Arizona, and a young woman, Sally, had stepped out of her everyday life to make me feel loved. This love and the readiness of my heart provided the perfect timing for my radical change. Almost immediately I wanted to go into ministry. I had such a heart to tell everyone what God had done for me.

But it wasn't quite time. Patience was involved.

God had to train me and prepare me for the things He would have me do later in my life, things I had no idea He would lead me to do. And wouldn't you know it, as soon as my vision was set for ministry, the doors opened for me to model! I was approached by a major department store and encouraged to pursue a modeling career. Now that my attention had shifted away from this career, the doors swung open wide for what I thought was my old vision. I prayed and asked the Lord what I was to do. He was telling me to go and be a light in an industry where a lot of darkness resides. I signed with one of the top agencies in Atlanta and went on with my life, assuming that it would take years for me to become active as a model and make a living at it.

The key to beholding YOUR vision is to first let go of your fear.

God's timing and order were much different than my own.

The day after I signed I received my first job offer. I had told the Lord I would honor Him by not taking any alcohol, tobacco, or lingerie advertisements. It was probably risky for the career path to rattle off this list of things I wouldn't do…especially to my agency. But I knew I had to stick to those personal convictions and my promises to God. When that first call came, I was ecstatic and listened nervously while trying to come across as cool when I spoke. My agent gave me the details of the job, and I was shocked to hear it was for a major beer campaign. The pay was huge, and I needed the money, but I knew it was a test. I gracefully declined and reiterated my conditions to my agent. It was never an issue again, and I worked regularly for six years modeling and acting. I was able to support myself on the income. I was on shoots for Macy's, Dillard's, *Seventeen* magazine, and for various commercials, and during the entire six years I evangelized the gospel to people who might not otherwise have heard it. I was where God called me to be, and I was thriving in His vision for my life.

Soon I had an opportunity to go to New York with a prestigious agency and pursue my career at a very serious level. I visited the city and got a taste for what my life would be like along this path—and I knew it was not what God had planned for me. I knew there was a greater purpose for why I was even in the modeling and acting world and that purpose was not for me to be a famous actress or model. I also had a burning passion to be a mother and have a family. That passion outweighed the thought of being famous or monetarily satisfied.

I declined this pursuit and went on to manage a retail store, worked in accounting and finance. Eventually my dream to marry and have children was fulfilled and during those wonderful child-rearing years I was still able to have fun doing commercials and print jobs. It would take some time, but eventually I understood exactly what was next for me and why I had gone through the experiences I had thus far. The modeling and acting had introduced me to the fashion industry, photography, style, and design—all the elements I need to create *Shine* magazine years later. The vision for this magazine and its ministry would have been shortchanged had it happened in my time, my order, my way. God was preparing me every step of the way, and He still is. The accumulation of things I had pursued along life's journey were all areas of expertise necessary for birthing the vision of *Shine* magazine.

All the things you've done in your life could play into the ultimate purpose God has for you. Each one of us is so uniquely different, and the plan God has for one woman will look very different than the plan He has for another. The key to beholding *your* vision is to first let go of your fear. You cannot hold on to both simultaneously. You may also have to release your hold on your personal vision because until you do, your hands will not be free to reach for what God brings to you next.

It comes right down to the purest belief of all for your God-crazy faith: "I can trust God." Many of us say that to others and to ourselves, but we also say it while one white-knuckled hand is clutching our old securities (or insecurities) for dear life. Or just pick any one of those pothole-causing behaviors, and chances are it is also going to cause a serious delay on your way to purpose. When you act in the mode of surrender, He will lead you, give you favor, and teach what you do not know. Don't let anything keep you from trusting God to give you wisdom in all you desire to do.

God Approved?

When I am speaking to a group, a question that comes up often from both men and women is, how can I know whether a vision for my life is of God or of my own desires? We all grapple with this, don't we? Sometimes our personal desires seem perfectly godly and righteous, yet we still cannot discern whether they are in line with God's calling.

So how *do* we know if our heart, our vision is God approved?

I believe spiritual maturity is a big factor. We need to be willing to pray and to wait and to listen as long as it takes before marching into the vision fully.

Vision Test

Here are the tests I use to see if the vision I have is really what God is calling me to or if it is my ego run amok. Just as we need to have our physical vision checked to be sure we are seeing without impairment, so we need to go through a spiritual vision exam when a dream, a goal, an ambition, or a purpose rises up in our mind and heart. Try these out.

1. *Will the pieces come together?* Sit back and throw the vision or the desire for vision out to God and ask Him to work on your behalf and to direct you toward what He wants to have done to launch the vision. For

example, if I need money, I wait for Him to bring it. If I need people, I wait on Him to bring me who I need. This doesn't mean you sit back and don't make an effort. It does mean that you wait patiently on the Lord and His timing and His resources. Don't aggressively force your will upon others or manipulate to get things done. Instead, allow things to unfold naturally and with a hands-off attitude. If you feel anxious and have no peace, I would take a step back and really pray to see if God wants you to move forward.

2. *Does it glorify God?* God is glorified when His Word is honored. Every vision must pass this test before you are able to take steps toward it.

3. *Are my motives pure?* It's fine if you personally benefit from the vision as long your objective is not solely about your personal benefit, but rather the advancement of the kingdom of God.

4. *Has God confirmed this vision through multiple sources?* Usually, if a vision is from God, He will speak to you through many ways, and you will have peace in your heart about it. If there is a lot of unrest, you will need to ask yourself why and continue to pray until you have a peace. Other means of confirmation will be comments and support from your closest spiritual friends and mentors. If they also bear witness to the vision, that is a strong validation. Sometimes God wants us to keep the vision to ourselves and not disclose it. Sometimes you are meant to keep it, hold it, protect it, and pray over it for a while.

5. *Is the vision time-tested?* Usually, when God has given you a vision, He will reinforce the vision in different ways and numerous times. For example, if it's in the form of a dream, it will reoccur. If it is in the form of a thought, it won't go away.

6. *Would you be willing to let it go?* If a vision is a promise of some sort from God, then usually He will have you die to it (be willing to let go of it) and leave it at the altar. Only if He resurrects it will it have His resurrection power behind it. That which God raises up, no man can tear down.

7. *Is there a supernatural peace that fills your heart?* Some visions involve a real step of faith on our part, but at the core of our being we have a peace that is beyond what our own confidence could bring. Usually, this is a strong signal that God is behind it.

8. *Can I walk in this with humility?* If you feel God has given you a vision, don't allow an attitude of self-righteousness to enter your heart. If God has really given you a vision to share, then preface your remarks by saying, "I believe God has given me a vision." After the fact of the vision coming to pass, it's okay to say, "It was God." No human being has an absolute, infallible connection with God. Again, there is room for error as we process life through sin and our own filters built in from years of our human experience. When God is speaking to us, it can get distorted. It is not wise to presume upon Him when it comes to visions. Walk in humility and see if the vision continues to rise up in your life.

9. *Is God providing or directing the resources, people, and wisdom for you to walk the vision out?* If He gives you a vision that involves stepping out in faith to do something, don't expect everyone in your life to rally behind you. Oftentimes, God is at work in your heart to purge you of fears. This does not mean that you have a martyr's complex about something. Again, stay humble, work quietly on the vision, and let God honor you or vindicate you in His time.

10. *Would you be willing to fail trying?* No vision will ever come to pass without this type of dedication. You must be willing to persevere. There will be many times when things won't make sense and you will have to put one foot in front of the other and trust God. He has never given me the entire picture of what I am to do. I just get pieces of the vision until finally I begin to see the bigger picture unfold. Another way to look at this part of the vision test is to ask yourself if you are willing to be afraid. Moving toward your vision could involve facing old fears. This tests our faith and keeps us completely dependent on Him so we do not rise up in pride.

Building the Résumé

It isn't easy to give up our expectation to be responsible (read: in control) of the means to the end result we desire. God's vision for us might very well counter the way we think and the way we are used to getting things done. Can you set aside preconceived ideas of what you think God wants and just allow Him to direct your path and equip you for the journey? You can make a plan, but you need to hold it loosely so God Himself is able to change it as He sees fit. The first thing to think about when it comes to vision or purpose is our life résumé.

Résumé? *Michelle, have you lost it? I don't want a job, I want a life of faith!* Ah, yes. But God builds résumés for different reasons and in very different ways than we do. Our list of accomplishments and achievements are likely to fall short of all we are capable of doing, but God's list of possibilities is beyond our imaginings and our current accomplishments. The only vision I had for myself when I was thrown out into the real world and no longer under my parents' roof was simply to be a wife and a mother. What a wonderful calling, and certainly the greatest accomplishment in my life, but God planted in me gifting and talent I didn't even know I had. When I surrendered my life to Him, He led me on a journey that eventually would act out my gifting and talent in ways I could *never* have imagined for myself.

The absolutely wonderful thing about the kingdom of God is the fact that it is available to all who desire it. There are no politics in heaven, no prejudices, no rich or poor. There are simply those people who love the Master, the Savior. Those who adore Him and desire to serve Him. The gospel is for everyone: the not-so-educated and the educated, those who are homeless and those who live in luxury, those who have not and those who have. But not all will hunger after it, not all will follow it, not all will give up everything to find it. Only those who truly seek Him shall find Him. The wonderful truth to this is that we all have an opportunity! We all have a chance. It doesn't matter where you grew up, who you grew up with, who you know, or who you don't know—the only one you need to know, the only contact you need is God. Yeah, this is great news! How inspiring it is to know you have a relationship with the Creator of this earth, and that He can take you wherever you need to go.

I love this truth about God's kingdom because in just about every other profession, organization, and even some ministries, everyone is more interested in your résumé than in you. It all comes down to this—let God build your résumé in living your life for Him. Release your grip on your life and let the Holy Spirit live through you. It is probably hard to think along these lines while living in a culture that teaches us to be interested in number one and to look out for ourselves over everyone and everything else. When you are focused on your divine audience of One, you aren't concerned with the way everyone else does things; you are concerned with the way God does things.

The difference in building a God-crazy résumé and building a résumé for self-gain is that our heart should be intent on building up things for the kingdom, not for ourselves here on earth. When this is the case, we will question every opportunity that comes our way and ask God, "Lord, is this a part of the plan You have for my life?"

Jonah Gets Kicked Off the Boat

I took a job a couple of years ago as editor of a national newspaper. I took the job for two reasons: It offered a huge monetary reward, and it would look great on my résumé and bring opportunities to me in the future. I didn't think twice about asking God what He thought or whether it was His will. I figured that since it was a Christian organization, it had to be God's will. Wrong. I started the job, and two weeks into it I realized it was not for me.

All of us can find an excuse to walk away from the purposes God has for our lives.

I felt like Jonah probably did when he was commanded by God to go to Nineveh. Instead of following this calling, Jonah followed his human confusion and fear and decided to get on a boat and go to Tarshish. Jonah's disobedience not only caused problems for him, but also for the men on the boat. The ship he had hopped on to get him to Tarshish was in peril of being torn apart by the sea, and once the men on board found out it was Jonah's disobedience to God that was causing their distress, they threw him off the boat, and he eventually ended up in the belly of a great fish for three days.

Once I took the job with the newspaper there was so much confusion. I had an overwhelming sense of anxiety. I couldn't think clearly, and ideas for the paper were not coming to me at all, and usually I can count on coming up with ideas. So even my usual gifting couldn't function. I knew if I stayed it would not be good for anyone because I was a traveler on the wrong boat going to the wrong place, and I didn't belong! Or in our tale of God-crazy exploration, you could say I was in the wrong car and I was trying to drive it myself. I went to the president of the company and resigned. He was not happy, but instantly a peace come over me that further confirmed my decision. Looking back, I know the decision was more than right on my part, and I am thankful I was sensitive enough to what God wanted for my life to move away from it regardless of the consequences. God gives us discernment, and we will know when and if we get off track from His plan, but only if we are openhearted to what He wants us to do with our time and our talents, and if we are willing to let Him build our résumé from start to finish.

After that experience I realized the importance of taking the time to evaluate every opportunity that comes my way. I no longer just jump into things hoping they are God's will. I think through decisions carefully, and I use the vision test to make sure each opportunity is in line with what God has called me to do. Sometimes the direction I should take is made known to me just by the feeling of peace I have over the situation. The great thing about God is that even if we get off track and move down a path that is not necessarily in line with His plan, He will work it for good, and we will grow from the situation. The Christian path is all about the learning, the growing, the believing, and the trusting.

I've used the example of an actual job for my résumé illustration…but the truth of how God works is applicable to every decision we make in life regarding every area of our lives. God builds a much better résumé—and a much better life—than we could ever hope for.

Are We Qualified?

If I had waited until I was qualified for anything I've ever done in my life, I might not have children, and I definitely wouldn't have worked in ministry as a leader for MOPS (Mothers of Preschoolers) or as a worship leader. I never would have had a radio program, women's magazine, book published, television program, and I'm sure I'm leaving something out here, but you get the point. Seriously, my résumé does not qualify me for any of the things I have stepped out in faith to do. God guided my steps, directed my heart leadings, led me toward opportunities, and gave me the peace to go forward and do all these things. I didn't try to force the direction or the timing. Sometimes it takes us years before we answer to a prompting God puts on our hearts, but hey, better late than never, right?

Look at the life of Moses and the conversation he had with God in the book of Exodus. When God called on Moses to take it to the next level in his adventure and purpose, Moses responds with, "Who am I that I should go to Pharaoh and bring the children of Israel out of Egypt?" (Exodus 3:11). God convinces Moses why he need not be afraid. God not only takes time to inform Moses that he will have the God of Israel on his side (which you think would be enough!), but He lays out every detail of the plan (wouldn't we all love that), and still, after God exhausts every reason for Moses to accept this place of honor, Moses' response is one of doubt. "Oh, my Lord, I am not eloquent, either in the past or since you have spoken to your servant, but I am slow of speech and of tongue" (Exodus 4:10). Then the Lord says to him something really great for us to hear today, "Who has made man's mouth? Who makes him mute, or deaf, or seeing, or blind? Is it not I, the LORD? Now therefore go, and I will be with your mouth and teach you what you shall speak" (Exodus 4:11-12).

Think on this comment from God, especially if you are a back-seat driver or a white-knuckler. We might have many opinions about where we are supposed to go or many worries, but is it not God who made us and who can teach us to be all that we were made to be? Well, like a lot of us, Moses heard the promises of the Lord and yet was still too afraid to believe...and he didn't want the job. He again responded in fear, "Oh, my Lord, please send someone else" (4:13). The passage goes on to say the Lord's anger was kindled, and He then assigned Aaron to help Moses so he wouldn't be afraid (verse 14).

How many of us have responded in the same way? We don't think we are eloquent enough or beautiful enough or gifted enough. All of us can find an excuse to walk away from the purposes God has for our lives. There will always be a reason, a distraction, or a weakness the enemy reveals to us in order to keep us thinking we are just not good enough for the job.

When the Lord called Moses, He knew Moses would feel inadequate. God knew He would be the source of strength in the areas Moses was weak. He knew there was no impairment that would keep Him from fulfilling His purposes for Moses and through Moses. The only obstacle was Moses himself, and the only potential obstacle in the way of God fulfilling His purposes in my life is me. I can so relate to Moses. In just about everything God has called me to, my first response has been, "Who me?" Seriously, I have even rattled off a few names of women I felt could do the job better. Yet the point we so often miss is that God doesn't give us things because He thinks *we* can do them, He gives us things *He* can do through us.

Shoes Much Too Big

One late night I was feeling extremely overwhelmed, which is how I feel most evenings when I am exhausted and there are mounds of laundry, a littered living room, and a stack of dirty dishes. God had really impressed on my heart a new vision. I was thrilled for the opportunity, but as usual was feeling quite inadequate for the calling. I described to a friend how I feel as though there are these shoes set out before me and they are three times my size, yet God is asking me to wear them and head out into the unknown. My good friend, who is very insightful, said to me, "Yes, this makes sense. If the shoes He gives you fit perfectly, why then would you need God to help you wear them? This way, you have to depend on Him every step of the way."

What a revelation. What a change in perspective with that simple response. I was a Christian at the time—I prayed, I relied on God for my needs to be met, but I hadn't changed my thinking to line up with this absolutely freeing, remarkable truth: We actually need God to help us fulfill our purpose. It's what He desires. It's how we are made. It's the way to God crazy! God wants us completely dependent on Him for each step of walking out the vision He has entrusted to us. What God doesn't want is for us to dwell on the inadequacies we think stand between us and the purpose He is nudging us toward. Why did Moses respond the way he did? Why couldn't he see himself the way God saw him? Surely most of us know the reasons because we have done the very same thing time after time. Maybe he had played that list of inadequacies over and over again in his head and allowed the enemy to convince him that they were what would keep him from God's best instead of being a built-in part of the man God was going to use for great purposes. Moses' weaknesses would magnify God's majesty.

But Moses was determined to believe more in his fears than he did in the strength of the Lord. It's the same way when we start fulfilling the purpose we have here on this earth. All the flaws that are so evident to us, our failures, and the sinful nature of our heart keep us thinking that we are somehow not good enough or qualified enough to fulfill His purpose and vision in our lives. How could He use me in my humanity, being the sinful person I am? How and why would He want to use me? Why doesn't He choose a better Christian? Everyone is afraid people will find out the real person inside, that their flaws will suddenly become evident to everyone. We are all the same, and there isn't a person who doesn't doubt their own abilities. But those of us who embrace God's ability and let go of our flawed vision will experience God's perfect vision for our lives.

God-crazy vision is simply putting your trust in God instead of placing your trust in yourself for your family, your future, and your life! We trust Him to build our résumé, to make up for our inadequacies, and to guide us in the direction we should go, and we stay open on the journey in case we need to detour off into an area He wants to grow us in. Detours are as important as the end result.

I had a friend recently tell me a story about a young girl who gave a presentation in which she showed a line as a symbol of the world and its affairs, and then she showed a dot representing God and His affairs. The question she asked the class at the end of her presentation was "Are we focused on the line or the dot?" Not bad for a young girl still in high school. Are we focused on the line, or are we focused on the dot? I think we have to ask ourselves this question every day because as much as we try to keep our sights steady on the dot, the line catches our attention. We can be thankful that God is patient enough to wait for us to get our focus back where it needs to be.

❧ La Vida Loca ❧

1. Prepare your heart to be open to a detour from your plans. Say yes to Him today and let Him know you are saying yes to whatever He has for your life.

2. How have you tested your visions and dreams in the past?

3. Which tests helped you understand the differences between our ways and God's ways?

4. Can you think of a time (or two) when you thought something was of God and it was purely of your own desires? What happened?

5. Let's face it—hindsight is always keener. But when you switch to resting in God's strength and His purpose, you will be amazed at how much better your spiritual vision will become. Keep track of those decisions and questions and directions you are facing now with this new godly perspective and heart. Keep track of what happens and how this time the journey feels different.

6. It's never too late to begin allowing God to build your résumé. Just stay open to Him and ask the Holy Spirit to direct your path.

7. Open your mind and heart to a different way of thinking, a new way of thinking…God-crazy thinking. Be open to new ideas and things you may not have thought of ever doing. You never know where God will

take you. He knows things you don't even know about yourself, and He knows what you are capable of.

8. Do you watch for the line or do your eyes stayed fixed on the dot representing God? God is everywhere...so why is it so hard for us to keep our focus on Him? What has distracted you most in your life?

9. Whatever distractions you thought of...be prayerful about them. Safeguard your life and your present and future purpose by giving these distractions over to God and by being accountable to someone in your life about them.

10. Make the switch to trusting God rather than relying on the tangible and human resources in your life. This is a tough one, but a very freeing one. Let God's vision unfold as you seek Him completely and without restrictive ties to your old priorities.

❖ GOD-CRAZY PRAYER ❖

Father, grant me a vision that is from You. Keep my eyes on You and Your face as I walk through the valleys and the peaks on the way through this God-crazy journey. Lay aside my personal desires so that I might adopt only Your desires for my life. Guide me, give me wisdom, and surround me with discerning believers who will also help me to test the visions and dreams and hopes I hold in my heart. I want to know they are of You and of Your will for my journey. I believe You have a special purpose for me, Lord. I am so very grateful. In Jesus' name. Amen.

10

LOVE'S POWER

When we yield ourselves to the power of the love of God,
He makes a masterpiece out of our mess, and as we receive
this grace in our lives we are then empowered to go into
the world and love others with a magnificent love.

—MICHELLE BORQUEZ

What does it mean to love with God-crazy love? Imagine it's early in the morning, and we are on the road.

The sun has just come up. God's behind the wheel, so you and I are free to sit and chat with no interruptions (can you imagine?). Stay with me just a moment, and let's think about Adam and Eve, and God's love for them. He loved them so much He gave them everything they would ever need. He forbade them one thing—and one thing only—to eat of the tree of the knowledge of good and evil. He reminded them that He was their Creator, their God, and that He had an express will for them. The tree itself was not evil, but the act of going against God's expressed will would introduce sin in the paradise of Eden, and beyond.

I can imagine the loveliness, the abundance, the breathtaking beauty of Adam and Eve's surroundings in the Garden, with color, texture, and scents offering them great pleasure and joy as they had communion with God. There probably wasn't even a lot of thought given to the one forbidden tree, or what life on the other side of the choice to go against God could look like.

Ah, but Satan knew how to woo them, how to seduce them by offering a mere counterfeit of what God had for them. Satan dangled two kinds of bait in front of Adam and Eve to cinch the deal. First was the visual temptation. The beautiful fruit was ripe, lush, lovely to the eye and to the touch, and especially appealing because it was forbidden. Satan presented it in such a way that Adam and Eve were certain that this fruit would lead them to a life of more than they had. This leads to the second bait, that of selfish ambition and agenda. The Garden couple had a glimpse of something they thought might be greater than immediate communion with God and obedience to God—the chance to become God or His equal. Satan planted the seed of distrust in them so that they would question God's motives and purpose.

Genuine love will not require others or yourself to perform because it is complete in itself.

Satan has not changed a bit. He dangles the same bait in front of us...something visually enticing or something that will appeal to our desire to be all-important, all-knowing, and in control of our own futures. We stand in God's presence, loving Him and grateful for the life we have...and then all of a sudden we have an encounter with the temptation, with the desire to have that which is not of God's will. It might be something we think we can't live without. It might be a direction or a decision that will lead us away from God's purpose for us. Let's face it...sometimes we reach for that forbidden fruit, completely forgetting about God's great love and His best for our circumstances.

When we choose the tempting fruit that is forbidden, whatever that happens to be in our lives, we are aware—we are given knowledge of—evil and its harsh contrast to the purity we had before this awareness. There is separation between us and God, and the gap becomes more and more painful. Any life apart from God is a life that sprouts dissatisfaction. When Eve looked around, she didn't see the lush trees, the rich soil, the beautiful shade trees, the brilliantly colored flowers. She looked around and thought, *I could do better. There is probably an even nicer garden on the other side of the valley.* Sound familiar? Have you become dissatisfied and disillusioned because God has not given you what you thought you should have? If we are inclined to take inventory of our life and consider what is missing, we will surely long to take matters into our own hands. It's our nature. Wanting a good life is fine, but following a counterfeit purpose instead of the real deal produces a temporary satisfaction that will still leave you longing for something more... authentic love.

What's Love Got to Do with It?

Satan has not stopped misrepresenting truth. The greatest lie of all, and the one that makes us consider swapping real purpose for fake treasures, is that God cannot, does not, or will not really love us for who we are. Have you ever believed this lie? Have you ever based decisions, choices, or your sense of worth on this lie? You will know if you are mapping out your life based on this great deception if you:

- Become anxious when you think you have lost control of a situation.

- Feel alone and experience a lack of intimacy.

- Take matters into your own hands instead of giving them to God.

- Rely on "positive thinking" instead of God's power.

- Make your life about obligation instead of passionate pursuit.

- Fear failure and become performance based.

- Feel dissatisfied with life and never fulfilled.

- Gossip about and rejoice in the failures and sins of others.

- Always wonder who is better than you because of pride.

- Avoid bringing decisions to God in prayer.

- Lack the wisdom of God's Word.

- Become self-centered with a personal, not eternal, agenda.

- Pursue idols instead of God.

- Will not share the gospel.

- Keep records of peoples' wrongdoings.

When you embrace the truth that God loves you, and you experience God's pleasure in the way you work, play, relate, think, pray, and love, nothing will compare. All will be deeper and more meaningful because it will be tied to more eternal purposes. The new nature of love that comes from this satisfaction is the perfect example of how God-crazy living is so different. This new love is selfless, engaged, dynamic, compassionate, kind, generous, and overflowing as it comes from the never-ending source of God's full love. Genuine love will not require others or yourself to perform because it's complete in itself. You don't need to keep proving your worthiness. This freedom infuses your perspective and intentions so thoroughly that you release the old guilt, pain, or selfishness and become open to love that surpasses worldly success and achieves eternal satisfaction.

When you have surrendered to the joy and wonder of God's unconditional, whole, healing, powerful love, you will:

- Have a growing ability to know God loves you.

- Trust that God cares about everything in your life.

- Feel forgiven and free of the bondage of sin because of Christ's love and His death.

- Have a broken and contrite heart.

- Take risks and even fail.

- Keep no records of wrongs and forgive those who hurt you.

- Be able to freely confess faults and mistakes.

- Trust in God's plan and purpose for your life.

- Be soul-satisfied by Christ.

- Long for others to know Christ.

- Rest in Christ and see love's victory over the flesh.

- Stand confident in Christ and see your self-worth and your identity.

Loving Ourselves

Loving ourselves begins with letting God's Word define who we are instead of allowing the world to define who we are. An understanding of our identity in Christ will influence our choices. If we hate ourselves, if we don't want good for ourselves, then a series of unhealthy choices will begin. It will become more and more difficult to respond to others out of a pure love. Learning to love ourselves, to forgive ourselves, to have mercy on ourselves, and to believe in ourselves is a step toward loving others.

I have spoken to many women who struggle to see their life as God does. It's so hard to love ourselves because we know what happens in our thought life and heart life, and it isn't always pure. Yet everyone struggles with the same issues. Satan can convince us we are unworthy, not good enough, a horrible person, and, worst of all, *unlovable.* I would say that Satan doesn't even need to do this because so many of us beat ourselves up and are quick to list our shortcomings and our failings. Pretty soon we are so sure of our failings that even if people compliment us or encourage us, we only hear a negative spin. And to add to the sense of isolation, we are convinced that nobody else feels this way.

I'll let you in on a secret…most of us have had that thought at one point or another. It has been difficult for me to learn to love myself. I spent most of my life not liking who I was, and the freedom that has come in accepting myself in my shortcomings, in my frailties, in my weaknesses, and in my failures has not been easy. But when God instructed us not to sit in judgment of anyone, He meant *anyone,* and that includes us. Loving ourselves takes a lot of prayer and reading of the Word because it is only here that we discover the truth about who we are and why God still loves us despite it all.

If we can make the jump from "I am not worth much" to "Christ died for me…for my sins and for my future eternity," there is a shiny new hope for us to claim. Yes, we are sinners, but Christ is our Savior. We are freed from sin and made worthy because of Him. We can embrace this truth fully, just as He embraces us fully. Feel the love!

❋ GOD-CRAZY MOMENT ❋

When I was in junior high, I attended a party for the band and choir members. I was thrilled to be going. At age 13 there wasn't much my parents would let me attend. They had recently become Christians and were bent on shutting everything worldly out of our lives. They reluctantly agreed to let me go. I felt their concerns were more about their newfound faith than any justifiable reason or wisdom.

Not too long after arriving at the party, the parents of the boy having the party left, and the only teens remaining were several boys, myself, and one other girl. She was a sweet girl, but unlike me, she was fully developed physically. I felt bad for her because all the boys made fun of her. There were rumors that she was less than prim and proper, but at the party her behavior seemed fine. We actually enjoyed a nice talk and had a lot of fun. When I got home I thought how attending the party had been a great decision.

But the next day at school I got wind of rumors being spread by the boys who had been at the party. They said the other girl and I had sex with all of them. I had not even kissed a boy in my life, so you can imagine how devastated I was. The injustice of this lie was more than my little mind could bear, and the lies bred a sense of shame that settled into my heart. Later, in high school, the boy who had started the horrible rumor apologized to me, and I forgave him, but the wound went so deep that even in my adult years the pain was vivid.

That same young man, after high school, went to jail for pulling a gun on another boy. By then I had a relationship with Jesus, so my compassion went out to him. I tried to find his address so I could tell him about Christ and his opportunity for a redeemed life through Him. Why was I compelled to forgive such a person and try to reach out to him? It's because I had the Lord's love for him. I saw this man as a soul who, in living without Christ, was capable of immorality and a life without the forgiveness I knew. The only difference between those who know Christ and those who don't is the fact that in our humanity Jesus is our source of love and our strength to overcome the temptations of the enemy. It's in His strength we are able to overcome and be made righteous.

Love's Honesty

Just think what would have happened if Adam and Eve had gone to God and said, "Father, tell us if what the serpent says is true. Will we be like You if we eat of the tree?" God would have shed truth on the lies, and His children could have overcome the temptation. Let's be honest with God. Tell Him how you feel. If you feel hate, then say, "I hate." If you feel unforgiveness, then say, "I cannot forgive." You can't hide anything from the Lord, so it's better to be honest so that you can receive His wisdom and guidance for your situation. Go to Him and open up your heart. "Lord, I need Your help to overcome and be able to get past this pain, despair, and betrayal I feel. I cannot do it in my own strength. It's too difficult. Please help me."

God created in us an unbridled passion to love and to be loved. Some of us have hardened our hearts or shut out love because of past wounds. We have decided we are unlovable ourselves, or maybe we just don't see how others could love us, or how God could love us. Regardless of what *we* think, we were made for love—to be loved and to love others.

When Jesus instructed us to love our enemies, to love our neighbors, to love others as we love ourselves, do you think He knew how difficult that would be? Do you think He understood that there would be times when we felt this was impossible? Of course He did. But He also understood then and now that with God all things are possible. It is only in His strength that we are able to love others, love ourselves, and most assuredly love our enemies.

In Romans 12, Paul makes it very clear that love should be genuine, instructing us to love one another with affection, even showing honor to one another. He goes on to say we should bless those who persecute us, associate with the lowly, and give our enemy food when he is hungry. Paul wrote of this ideal, godly love from prison. From confinement and a place of persecution he presented a love so revolutionary that to this day it is pursued and longed for. It is Christ's revolutionary love.

Loving Beyond What Is Required

How are we as believers in Christ different from the world? How does Christ demonstrate love in His Word? Recently a friend of mine and I were driving through a grocery parking lot, and an older lady set out to cross in front of us but was still far enough away from us that my friend chose not to stop. Still, I asked him why, and he spent a few minutes justifying his actions.

We got out of the car and went inside the store to do a little shopping. While checking out the grocery checker seemed over-whelmed. It was busy and he had nobody bagging groceries. I asked my friend if he could help bag the groceries so I could write my check. By the look he gave me I could tell he was not thrilled with my request. When we got out to the car I asked him why he had looked at me the way he did when I asked him to bag the groceries. His response included, "It's not my job. The store is a high scale one, and they make enough to have someone bag your groceries." I could see once again his justification for his actions. My friend was not wrong in his remarks either time, but he was doing what we all often do—we think about what is fair and what is required, and nothing beyond that.

When we talked about it, I felt convicted in my own life. How many times do I drive around getting frustrated with people on the road who, I'm convinced, should have their license revoked? Sure, I would have stopped for the lady, and I would have bagged the gro-ceries, but am I patient with the person on the highway who isn't driving fast enough for me? If we are only committed to do what is required of us how will anyone ever see the love of Christ lived out on this earth? Love is often about doing more than what is required; it's also about sacrifice.

When I see a little old lady in the parking lot trying to get her groceries in the car, is it my job to help her? When I pass by a home-less family on the street, is it my job to feed them? When I hear about a single woman in need of help to provide for her family, am I required to give? I can offer up many reasons to justify not doing any of these things, but here is the best reason for why I *should*. If I do not have the heart of God for others, if I do not display the love of Christ by helping with my hands and speaking encouragement with my mouth, then who will, how will anyone see who God truly is?

Going beyond what is required of us is shocking to people in our culture. When we take time to help someone without wanting anything in return, when my friend helps bag groceries even though it's not his job, when I stop and help a mom in the parking lot who has more than she can handle, when I encourage a woman in the bakery to take time for herself, I am spreading the love of Christ, and believe me, this is noticed and people are changed by it.

Unconditional Grace

God instructs us not to judge lest we be judged, and yet our first instinct when we hear of someone's failure is to judge them. Haven't we all done this? When we are drawing our strength from our relationship with the Lord, judgment will no longer be our first response. Love will override this very human desire to assess another's behavior in order to feel better about ourselves or to feel more powerful. Love will call us to lay out the fruit of that person's actions and allow the Spirit of God in us to discern how to gently respond to their pain, their sin, and their heart.

It's not easy sharing shameful secrets, is it?

We are often the hardest on other believers, practically kicking them when they are down instead of lifting them off the ground and helping them to walk again. We are all sinners, and some of us get caught in the mire of sin and find ourselves in a place where we could use another believer to help us get out of the muck, yet we are often afraid to expose our sin. This has got to stop if we are going to see people freed from the shackles of sin, especially hidden sin. With the Internet, iPods, and cell phones, we are able to sin in our own private worlds without anyone knowing it, and yet God knows it. Sin rises up to surround our hearts and minds and spirits in a prison for believers and unbelievers alike, but the believer can turn to the Lord and seek refuge and healing. The one caught up in sin's snare should be able to turn to another believer and ask for help. If your sister was walking along a road with you and fell into a ditch, wouldn't you attempt to reach down for her and pull her up out of her circumstance? Why then, when our sister or brother in Christ falls, do we often walk away, as if their sin is contagious or as if we are blameless in our human condition?

When I was around ten, a cousin and I found some of my grandfather's pornography magazines. We sat out in my grandparents' truck looking through them, filled with curiosity. It was the first time I had ever seen pornography, and even though no one had ever talked to me about it, I knew it was wrong to be looking at it. We were found out, and the whole family made such a big deal over it that we were both deeply shamed. I felt there was something wrong with me because of how the adults responded. There was no moment of grace. And instead of separating the sin from me, they lumped everything together without explanation. I thought I was so bad and so past redemption because of their response to the porn. I wish someone had pulled me aside and reinforced their love for me and defined the sin as separate from the sinner. My cousin and I laugh about it today, but at the time it was so hurtful.

Finally brothers, rejoice. Aim for restoration, comfort one another, agree with one another, live in peace; and the God of love and peace will be with you.

2 Corinthians 13:11

Shaming people in their sin, further condemning them, and casting them out is not the love God spoke of in His Word. Instead, we are to come alongside our brothers and sisters, as well as unbelievers, and offer them the cloak of overcoming rather than the cloak of shame.

When I think of God's grace in my life, the infinite grace He has shown me over and over again, I am humbled. There are so many times I have been blessed by His forgiveness and mercy, but one very personal example stands out. I hadn't planned to share this story in this book, but it is such an important part of my understanding of

God's grace. I remember the first time God asked me to share about having an abortion. I told the Lord, "I can't. I don't want people to think I am not perfect, not together, not faithful." The Lord quickened my spirit and spoke to me again. "Michelle, when you share with women about the things I have done in your life, who do you want them to see? Are you wanting them to see you, or do you want them to see what I have done through you?" I had to think about that for a moment. It's not easy sharing shameful secrets, is it? But God removes our guilty stains, the shame is replaced with His abundant grace, and we are able to lift our head and face the world again.

When I was in my late teens, I had a boyfriend who was the first love of my life. I became pregnant on his prom night and felt there was no way I could ever face my dad with the news. I was not saved at the time, but I don't say that because it had anything to do with my decision. Even when we are saved, when we fall into sin, the first thing we seek to do is cover that sin up and hide our shame.

Years later I went through a healing process and God used me to minister to young girls contemplating abortion, but still the guilt I carried as a result surfaced when I married and began to want a family. My husband and I began trying for children, and when I didn't get pregnant the first month I immediately thought it was a result of my sin. I began to think about my life without children, and I accepted my sentence thinking God was justified in not allowing me the privilege and joy children would bring to my life. I even thought of ways I could serve Him instead of being a mother. I could be a businesswoman and impact the business world. Well, thank God for His grace, His mercy, and His forgiveness. I am so very grateful this is not the way He operates. One month later I found myself pregnant, and if that were not enough, I had four children in five years. They are all not only healthy, but they are highly intelligent and have great personalities. And the joy they give me, even when they mess up, is a constant reminder of how dearly and unconditionally God loves His children.

Not only does God forgive the repentant heart, but He graces us with His beautiful mercy like water washing over us. We are clean, and He has forgotten all our sin. When I first became a Christian, I felt God leading me to write down, over and over: "I am no longer the girl of my past, I am no longer the girl of my past, I am no longer the girl of my past." Do I feel sorry for the choice I made? I feel deeply, desperately sorry, but I know God has it covered, and I know He knew all the mistakes I was going to make up until this point, and yet in His sovereignty He has chosen to use me regardless. He is going to use you regardless. His love for you knows no boundaries. There is nothing His blood does not cover. I have dedicated all my children to the service of the Lord. When I was able to have my first baby, my son Joshua, I knew God loved me beyond what I could even fathom.

When we reach for Jesus and the absolute truth of His love, we will be given the ability to overcome.

> "Do not let your hearts be troubled. Trust in God; trust also in me. In my Father's house are many rooms; if it were not so, I would have told you. I am going there to prepare a place for you. And if I go and prepare a place for you, I will come back and take you to be with me that you also may be where I am. You know the way to the place where I am going." Thomas said to him, "Lord, we don't know where you are going, so how can we know the way?" Jesus answered, "I am the way and the truth and the life. No one comes to the Father except through me. If you really knew me, you would know my Father as well. From now on, you do know him and have seen him" (John 14:1-7 NIV).

Jesus brings our troubled hearts peace. God shows us the way to covenant with Him throughout eternity in the life and the death and the resurrection of Christ. The truth we need, the love we long for from the moment we are born, and the way we need to go to know our purpose and love's transforming power is all found in Christ.

Wouldn't it be wonderful if we actually became so God crazy that people would feel unconditional love from us and be transformed forever? The love and compassion we receive from Christ, and that we can pass along to others, does indeed transform people's lives, just as it did our own. That is why God called us to love in this way—in His way—so people would see Jesus in us and want to engage in His embrace the same way we have.

When we fall head over heels for His way—*the* way—and His heart, and we hold on to all that is of God, we don't need or desire those lies that change the course of our surrendered paths. We can rest in the absolute, undeniable power of love that God pours out onto His children.

We no longer need validation from others, but instead we seek and find validation from Him. If we seek our security in what others think of us, we will never feel accepted or loved. Our security can only come from knowing His love for us. When we realize this truth, we are able to live out the God-crazy life.

We are simply the vessel in which God chooses to use to be His hands, His feet, and to speak His message to people everywhere… nothing more. We are the vessel God uses to display His magnificence to others, and what a wonderful privilege we should count it to be used by Him to do so.

—MICHELLE BORQUEZ

❧ La Vida Loca ❧

1. Do you really understand and accept God's love for you?

2. What are some ways you have seen God show His love to you?

3. Do you love yourself? Where do you seek your validation? If from others, then ask yourself why?

4. Have choices you've made been a result of the perspective you have of yourself?

5. Can you recall times you based decisions on the lie that God doesn't love you? What happened? How did that lie take hold of your heart at that time?

6. How can drawing nourishment from God's Word help you grow in love?

7. What are some ways you can better love others and help them get through the process of failures and sin?

8. Are you judgmental? If so, why?

9. How do you get beyond judgment and move into mercy and compassion?

10. Have you been shamed? Have you moved beyond it? If not, have others pray for you so that you are able to be free from shame.

❧ God-Crazy Prayer ❧

*D*ear Lord, help me to see myself as You see me. I long to be confident in Your love for me. Help me to love myself and to have mercy on myself the way You have mercy on me. Help me to have grace and compassion for myself and to take time to rest. Lord, give me wisdom to help others in their pain and their failures. Give me love for those who are unlovable and for those who do not yet know You. Help me to forgive those who have hurt me, shamed me, or rejected me. Keep me from being judgmental, and bring the Holy Spirit into my life so I am able to discern the hearts of others and love them beyond their sin. Thank You, Lord, for loving me and for showing me a revolutionary love that can change lives, including my own. In Jesus' name. Amen.

What Is This Love?

*What is Your love, Lord, that You would know
me in the very depths of my soul?*

*What is this love that breaks through the walls of
my hardened heart?*

*What is this love, Lord, that You would know
me and yet still love me?*

*Your love, O Lord, is vast. Like the ocean is to the land,
so Your love is to my heart—*

*Connecting at the very center of who I am.
I am humbled by this love You have for me.*

I am amazed at Your grace poured out over my life.

*My face covered with ashes, my emotion a bruised reed,
my life laid out before You broken, yet Redeemed and
washed clean by Your tremendous love for me.*

*What is this love that has chosen me and placed a
foundation of peace within my soul?*

How could I ever repay for this love I have found in You?

*There is no wealth or greatness that compares to the
love You have sewn inside my heart!*

It is in You that I find meaning on this earth.

Thank You, O Lord, for Your great love. Amen.

—Michelle

11

VICTIM VS. VICTOR

*Do not fear for I am with you; do not be dismayed, for I
am your God. I will strengthen you and help you; I will
uphold you with my righteous right hand.*

ISAIAH 41:10 NIV

I accepted Christ 20-something years ago. I experienced a radical
conversion from a life of darkness to a life in the light, and in this
more than 20-year journey God has slowly taken the broken pieces
of my life and redeemed each and every one. If God were to come
in and heal us from everything at one time, I believe it would crush
us. Instead, He slowly awakens us to the areas of our lives that have
not yet surrendered to Him, and then in His patience and loving
nature He fills us up with more of His Spirit, so we can then go and
be an instrument of healing to others.

While I was doing my best to ignore well-meaning loved ones
hoping to transform me, I was still forced to look at God's Word
as a form of truth, as a possibility for a greater life, but I did not
embrace or reach for Christ until I was at the very end of myself and
had exhausted every likelihood for happiness apart from God.

Only when we have become tired of playing the victim in our
own stories are many of us willing to reach for victory in Christ.
You are going to feel so much lighter after we drop the troubles

of past mistakes, repeated sins, and the burden of fending off the enemy with our own devices. You will feel renewed as together we embrace the wonder of living freely in God's protective covering of grace and goodness.

Living in the Spirit

So Jesus said to the Jews who had believed in Him, "If you abide in my word, you are truly my disciples, and you will know the truth, and the truth will set you free" (John 8:31-32).

Living as a victim is to live in and rely on the flesh. This gets us in trouble. When we forget that our power is in God, in His strength and might, we become that victim over and over again. A God-crazy woman rests in God's power to fight her battles.

A victim chooses to:	A God-crazy woman chooses to:
Reject truth	Embrace truth
Renounce truth	Speak truth
Rebuke truth	Will truth
Resist truth	Act in truth
Rebel against truth	Become truth

A victim feels:	A God-crazy woman feels:
Anxious	Confident
Worthless	Competent
Incompetent	Significant
Insignificant	Successful
Unacceptable	Secure
Hopeless	Worthy
Helpless	Loved
Unloved	
Used	
Depressed	
Uncertain about self and God	

God will reveal to you areas He needs to work on when it comes to unforgiveness, bitterness, jealousy, envy, insecurity, etc. He will reveal to you things over time that need to be restored. He is all about restoration, so don't give up. There is so much hope in Christ.

What can give us cause for doubt about living in faith is that we can react in the flesh and still get positive results. We hear "think positive" and "think good thoughts," and this all seems fine and righteous. However, when we change our thoughts and reactions toward the positive but still depend on ourselves, we are creating a shaky foundation. Our strength, our confidence, our competence, our significance, our success, our security, our worthiness, our love-

When we choose to go the road of the victim, we will end up disappointed and defeated every time.

liness should all be a result of our relationship with Christ and our ultimate dependence on Him for everything.

Remember, if you are getting your needs met apart from Christ, you are living a life in the flesh, which results in dead works. Dead works is a harsh term, but it makes perfect sense. A dead pear tree cannot give you ripe, juicy fruit to enjoy with your spinach salad. You can go out and look at that broken tree, with crumbling branches lying at its roots, and hope for a baby-smooth piece of fruit that is county-fair worthy, but there's no way you're going to get that. You might have firewood for a season, but that's as much as this tree will offer. If we keep going back to sources that are not alive in Christ and expect to find nourishment and fulfillment, then we are mistaken, misled, and headed for disappointment—and we are primed to fall victim to the enemy's traps and our own unhealthy behaviors, which grow zero fruit in our lives.

We are going to explore how Christ and His victory over sin offer you the way to your purpose and your daily living. Revisit that list of how a victim feels. How many of those items resonate with your emotional health today? Now take a look at how the God-crazy woman feels. This list is what we will work toward in this chapter and from here on out.

Following Jesus' Victory

When Satan worked hard to tempt Jesus with every area of the flesh, Jesus refused to give in to it. He embraced the truth of God, and He spoke out to the one striving to break Him.

> Jesus was led by the Spirit into the desert to be tempted by the devil. After fasting forty days and forty nights, he was hungry. The tempter came to him and said, "If you are the Son of God, tell these stones to become bread." Jesus answered, "It is written: 'Man does not live on bread alone, but on every word that comes from the mouth of God.'" Then the devil took him to the holy city and had him stand on the highest point of the temple. "If you are the Son of God," he said, "throw yourself down. For it is written: 'He will command his angels concerning you, and they will lift you up in their hands, so that you will not strike your foot against a stone.'" Jesus answered him, "It is also written: 'Do not put the Lord your God to the test'" (Matthew 4:1-7 NIV).

Jesus takes action against the enemy by reciting truth out loud. It is important we speak out as warriors for truth and against evil when temptation comes and we are unable to resist, or when trials come and we are unable to see a way out.

> Again, the devil took him to a very high mountain and showed him all the kingdoms of the world and their splendor. "All this I will give you," he said, "if you will bow down and worship me." Jesus said to him, "Away from me, Satan! For it is written: 'Worship the Lord your God, and serve him only.'" Then the devil left him, and angels came and attended him (Matthew 4:8-11).

Jesus willed Himself to stand against the enemy, and He then acted on the truth and fulfilled His purpose in ministry on this earth. This is what enabled the ministry of Jesus to be effective. It was His decision to be the victor God had purposed Him to be. When we choose to go the road of the victim, we will end up disappointed and defeated every time. The enemy comes to "steal and kill and destroy" (John 10:10). These are all active words, not passive words, and they are aggressive as well. The enemy is aggressive, and if we remain passive, it's easy to feel defeated.

Faith-Defense Class 101

As important as it is for women to become self-defense savvy to protect ourselves physically, we must also be faith-defense trained to protect ourselves from spiritual attacks. Welcome to the class that every God-crazy woman should take: Faith-Defense 101. If we combine some commonsense self-defense tactics and wisdom from Christ's example we read in Matthew 4, we can be victorious when we face those tempters, influencers, or obstacles that in the past have kept us as victims.

Be Prepared

Boy Scouts have it right when it comes to the best first rule in life: be prepared. When we arm ourselves with knowledge, God's truths from Scripture, and the power of Christ, we are preparing ourselves to no longer be victims and to move through the God-crazy life with a strong spiritual empowerment. Notice how in the reading from Matthew, Jesus responds to the taunts and challenges of Satan several times by saying, "It is written" and referring directly to God's Word.

Now, if Jesus is pulling out Scripture as part of His defense against the temptations of the enemy, then certainly this should also be our first line of defense. When we are grounded in God's Word, we are able to respond with godly strength to any tempter or temptation. Here are some promises in Scripture that will build up your sense of identity and purpose and Christ.

ACCEPTANCE
I am God's child. (John 1:12)
I have been justified. (Romans 5:1)
I am bought with a price. (1 Corinthians 6:19-20)
I have access to God through the Holy Spirit. (Ephesians 2:18)
I have been redeemed and forgiven. (Colossians 1:14)

I AM SECURE
I am free from condemnation. (Romans 8:1-2)
I cannot be separated from the love of God. (Romans 8:35-39)
I have not been given a spirit of fear, but of power, love and a sound mind. (2 Timothy 1:7)
I am born of God and the evil one cannot touch me. (1 John 5:18)

I AM SIGNIFICANT
I am the salt and light of the earth. (Matthew 5:13-14)
I am a branch of the true vine, a channel of his life. (John 15:1,5)
I have been chosen and appointed to bear fruit. (John 15:16)
I am a personal witness of Christ and His actions. (Acts 1:8)
I am a minister of reconciliation for God. (2 Corinthians 5:17-21)
I can do all things through Christ who strengthens me. (Philippians 4:13)

Build Strength

Work up those spiritual muscles and protect yourself with the armor of God. When we are faced with any kind of adversity and we go to flex our spiritual muscles and there is nothing...it leaves us cornered unless we are clothed fully in the armor of God. We can be dressed in His protection when we:

- Know and love His Word.

- Become aware of the enemy's tactics.

- Seek the ways of truth.

- Have a humble and righteous heart.

- Embrace a God-crazy commitment to peace.

Be strong in the Lord and in the strength of his might. Put on the whole armor of God, that you may be able to stand against the schemes of the devil. For we do not wrestle against flesh and blood, but against the rulers, against the authorities, against the cosmic powers over this present darkness, against the spiritual forces of evil in heavenly places. Therefore take up the whole armor of God that you may be able to withstand in the evil day, and having done all to stand firm. Stand therefore, having fastened on the belt of truth, and having put on the breastplate of righteousness, and, as shoes for your feet, having put on the readiness given by the gospel of peace. In all circumstances take up the shield of faith, with which you can extinguish all the flaming darts of the evil one; and take the helmet of salvation, and the sword of the Spirit, which is the word of God, praying at all times in the Spirit, with all prayer and supplication (Ephesians 6:10-18).

We would be wise to follow the U.S. Marines and say *semper fidelis*—always faithful—for it is by faith we will please our God. It is by faith we will endure the trials before us, it was by faith Jesus was able to overcome the temptations of Satan, and it is by our faith and His strength that we are able to resist the flesh and walk in the Spirit.

We can walk in faithfulness till the end, but only if we are equipped for battle. The Word of God is the only offensive and aggressive weapon when it comes to the armor of God. Put on the full armor of God in order to fight the fight. This is a daily task we must mentally embrace so we are able to stand strong in the life God created just for us.

There are many examples throughout my life where my parents have stood in the gap for either myself or one of my siblings, but I think the most fervent time, the occasion that probably caused them to really stand on His Word, was when my sister and I were in rebellion. They really held firm to "train up a child in the way he should go, even when he is old he will not depart from it" (Proverbs 22:6). I am sure that one verse alone helped them to have faith beyond what they were seeing in our lives. It was gut-wrenching for them to watch their two daughters live out the prodigal life and to have no control over it, but their determination to believe God's Word eventually led to our deliverance from the sin we had been living in, and ultimately our salvation. There may be some of you who are believing God for a loved one. Don't give up. Stand firm on His Word. His Word does not return void, and the power of it is limitless.

Reduce Risks

Experts and most any friend with common sense will tell you that your best chance of not becoming a victim is to avoid the risk to begin with. In straight talk: Don't make dangerous choices, be aware of your surroundings, and avoid walking in the dark. Let's follow the same wisdom for our journey of faith.

When we make decisions based on God's will, we will avoid many of the pitfalls we'd walk right into if we depended on our human insight. There is less chance for our wants to override our good judgment if we keep measuring our decisions against God's best for us.

Keep your eyes on God's purpose for your life. This awareness will help you determine which things are of Him and His will. There is such comfort in knowing when to say yes to things and when to say no to them. You will reduce your risk of overloading yourself to the point of ineffectiveness if you stay aware of what is of God and what is merely a distraction that can lead you astray. Sometimes these distractions are material possessions, a desire for success, or opportunities that at first seem very in line with God but are really intended for someone else or for you later on in your journey.

Avoid those dark places where your greatest temptations await you. Avoid corners shrouded in secrecy because they are likely filled with trouble. The way I see it, avoiding the dark in our spiritual adventure is our way to stop testing ourselves and God over and over again. When we repeat the same sins, the same mistakes, and still return to darkness rather than turning toward things of light and hopefulness, then we are testing God's faithfulness unnecessarily. In Matthew 4:7 when Satan tells Jesus to throw Himself from the heights so that angels sent by God will save Him, Jesus replies, "Do not put the Lord your God to the test" (NIV).

> *God-crazy women pack a mighty whop because they carry with them the power of Jesus' mighty name.*

Believe it or not, by adding a touch of wisdom to your experience, you can still have a very carefree adventure...in fact, it will be even more carefree when you stop saying "catch me" and just start living the God-crazy life filled with complete trust in God's direction and protection without having to test it constantly with unhealthy behavior and decisions.

De-escalate

Any mother knows the chill that goes up and down the spine when a child's emotional letdown escalates into an all-out breakdown. God must feel this a hundredfold when we fuel minor sins into infernos of destruction in our situations. If we are facing off with the enemy, if we are standing in front of one of our temptations that can easily snowball (like gossip or binging or throwing around a white lie), then we have a chance to embrace God's truth in that moment and keep our sin under control. Again, the verses we read earlier in Matthew help us out. We can see how to de-escalate a moment when facing off with the tempter.

The tempter came to him and said, " 'If you are the Son of God, tell these stones to become bread.' Jesus answered, 'It is written: "Man does not live on bread alone, but on every word that comes from the mouth of God" ' " (Matthew 4:3-4 NIV).

Jesus counters the invitation to sin, to give Himself over to Satan's influence, with godly wisdom and by standing firmly on the foundation of God's Word. When we first lean on God's understanding of what we need, then we avoid giving our temptation an ounce of consideration. There is not a chance for it to further tempt us because the subject is closed and our hearts are protected.

The God-crazy adventure will present you with new opportunities, beginnings, and open doors just waiting for a confident, transformed you to walk through. If, in the past, you have faced such open doors with fear and trepidation because of self-doubt, now the peace of Christ will rise up in your mind before you can spin your worries into huge obstacles. The path will be cleared for a fabulous journey!

Speak Up

"Away from me," Jesus calls out to Satan (Matthew 4:10 NIV). He rebukes the power and the presence of the enemy. We can do this in our own lives. To be spiritually safe, it is best to guard our hearts and minds by speaking out and rebuking any sin that comes our way. God-crazy women use their voices to convey God's strength when a challenge stands between them and their path to purpose. We are passionate beings who are quick to call on the name of the One we love and who loves us. We are never alone as we walk forward in God's will. If we falter, if we step off the path and come across the tempter, we can draw on the strength of the Lord. God-crazy women pack a mighty whop because they carry with them the power of Jesus' mighty name.

Ask for Help

Women accomplish many tasks in a day and often take care of

the needs of others. We set goals, reach milestones, support friends and family members, volunteer for things we believe in, and strive to be our best, but it's not always easy to ask for help when we need it, even when we need it desperately. Asking for help should be obvious, but it can be tough for us to do so.

I've told you about a few times when I have relied greatly on the kindness of a mentor or a prayer warrior, but I also confessed to facing my darkest hours often alone because I was afraid of looking imperfect or like a bad Christian. I'm so thankful I have learned to counter those old worries. I realized I could admit to sin or confess to weakness and people would still love me. God would still call me His own. This was an incredible relief, and it taught me to never place my pride over my spiritual well-being.

As we learn to seek help when we need it (and even when we think we don't) through prayer, accountability with others, a community of fellowship, and connection with mentors, we learn to safeguard our walk of faith. God's response becomes our covering, our shelter.

Walk with Confidence

Right after Jesus' battle with the enemy, He began His ministry. This is not just a random order of happenings. It is important for every God-crazy woman to pay attention. Jesus faced His most personal, head-on confrontation with Satan, and after He made it through, He went on to His ministry. My friend, when you are facing your most difficult times of darkness, challenge, and doubt... when you are facing your most personal, head-on confrontation with the enemy, you can walk with confidence through the fire. You will be ready, prepared, and anointed for the purpose ahead.

We will be tempted and have trials on this earth, I can assure you of this, but if we are prepared to walk into battle with the enemy, it can be a faith-affirming experience rather than a destructive one. It's important that we understand that when we step out to live the God-crazy life, we are most certainly in an ongoing battle. We just happen to know the One on high, and He is on our side and prepared to help us through it all. Not only do we end up on the other side of the battle, but we end up better prepared for our own purpose, ministry, and victorious life.

If it were not for three Baptist ladies who were living out the Word of God in their lives, passionate enough to knock on my Aunt Brenda's door and share with her the Word of God, that she in turn shared in a letter to my mother, Sandy, I would not have my heritage of faith or any relationship with Christ. When we get passionate about our victory in Him, we then want to live out His purpose and share it with others. For each passionate person who rises to their calling and gifting, many lives will be changed as a result.

Acknowledge the past and today's echoes of the past as part of the process of God's handiwork in your life. God has written off your mistakes, and He has accepted the burden of your pain. There is no longer any reason to consider yourself a victim. Because of His love, we are able to display His splendor in us, going out and being the church to those around us, loving unconditionally those in sin and those struggling with difficult life issues, and we are able to love them through the process because we love God with all our heart, and we also love ourselves.

So, girls, get God-crazy, and let God fill the corners of your life that cobwebs have resided in. He can transform us and His Word is truly alive! No longer strive and live exhaustedly, but instead soar with the beautiful wings of the eagle you were born to be! Don't put God crazy on your to-do list, but rather embrace the words in this book and let them become your life. Wake up every day refreshed and new, wondering what God is going to do next, wondering what surprises are right in front of you. Believe me, He has many surprises for you, and so much He wants to still do in your heart...if you will let Him.

❧ La Vida Loca ❧

1. Do you tend to define yourself with victim words rather than using victorious God-crazy language? Which words do you want to strike from your vocabulary?

2. Which words from the God-crazy list represent the characteristics you want most to embody?

3. What, in your past, seemed to defeat your spirit, your hopes, your dreams? Have you relied on God to overcome these? What still haunts you and impacts you today?

4. Have you thought of yourself as a victim recently? Was it because of someone else's behavior, your own, or the result of circumstances?

5. Look up those Scriptures that help you define your identity and strength in Christ. Journal how each of these make you feel.

6. How could you have reduced the risk of falling to temptation recently? Think through your decisions, emotions, and the end result. What would you do differently now?

7. Have you allowed a sin or situation to escalate when you could have relied on God to resist the temptation altogether? Chances are, that sin will rise up again. What will you do to stop it from becoming a greater obstacle?

8. Do you fear your own voice and power as a woman of God? You should take pride in the fact that you are His child and that you speak from this identity of both humility and power. Speak up and say...what? What do you want to say to your biggest stumbling block and to your life?

9. When is it hardest for you to ask for help? Why is it

difficult? Is there something from your past or your present that keeps you from reaching out? Discover what stops you from asking for assistance from God, others, and your own wisdom. Be very aware of these and pay attention to what stops you from asking for help the next time you need it. Freeing yourself from the desire to do it all alone will also free you to embrace God's purpose for you.

10. Can you let go of the past? Can you let go of your troubles today? Can you accept with great joy the transformation that awaits you when you rest in His Word and surrender to Him completely? List out your fears, and then list out your hopes for your new life.

❧ GOD-CRAZY PRAYER ❦

Savior, I come to You with all my fears, my worries, my sins, and my transgressions, and I ask You to turn these human losses into victory in You. Make my weakness all about Your strength. Show me how to embrace truth and renounce the maker of temptations so that I do not fall away from this amazing purpose You have given to me. I no longer have to live in the dark shadows, afraid of what might come my way. I have the strength of Your might. I can take on the whole armor of Your truth and saving grace, Lord. I love You with all that I am, God. Thank You for the example we have in Jesus' life. There is nothing, not even death, for me to fear because You have conquered all. I celebrate this victorious life, and I am more God crazy than ever! In Your precious, powerful name. Amen.

12

THE HEART OF PRAYER

Rejoice always, pray without ceasing,
and give thanks in all circumstances; for this is the
will of God in Christ Jesus for you.

1 THESSALONIANS 5:16-18

One Sunday morning during the church class for young married couples, our teacher asked those who needed prayer to raise their hand. I slowly raised mine and then quickly put it down, fearful he might actually call on me. As he went around the room listening to various prayer requests, I battled my shyness for a few moments, trying to rally the courage to raise my hand and speak my request. With my stomach in knots, I finally blurted out my prayer need. Whew! What a relief. I had done it. Can you imagine getting all worked up over communicating a prayer request in a group? Maybe you've experienced the same feelings I did or at least hesitated to express your heartfelt needs even in a caring community. While this happened many years ago, the memory of fear and trepidation is vivid. Back then I would become a ball of nerves at the mere thought of having to pray, speak, or give requests in a group.

As I look back at those times, I realize that my problem with prayer extended beyond the public arena and into my personal, private communication with God. My prayer life at home was lackluster, if not flat out lacking, because I had allowed the enemy to convince me my requests were unimportant. I prayed my prayers with uncertainty and even apologetically because I didn't want to bother God with my offerings and concerns. I deeply loved the Lord, yet when I closed my eyes and lifted up my heart to Him, I hoped rather than firmly believed that He would hear me. It was difficult to believe that God truly cared about me and my concerns. I mean, I watched the evening news and knew all about serious hardships and tragedies taking place daily. Why would God lean a listening ear in my direction? The only time I felt I had something worth hearing was when I was in a desperate situation of some kind. According to George Barna in his book *The Revolution,* half of all believers say that in the past year they do not feel they have entered into the presence of God or experienced a connection with Him.

Passionate, authentic prayer requires us to believe beyond what we see.

Is it God or us? (I'll give you one guess.)

Is it our method of prayer or our inability to set aside our self-consciousness and self-awareness long enough to be vulnerable and humble before our God? If we come before the Lord as though we are insignificant to Him, then I wonder if we have much faith to begin with.

Going through the motions of our religion rather than engaging in the rich practices, disciplines, and privileges of our personal faith is like peddling a bike whose chain has become detached from the wheel. We exert a lot of effort only to find ourselves in the same place we were when we started. We become frustrated and possibly even angry and disenchanted with the desire to grow in relationship with Christ. In many of the Christian circles I've been involved in, I've witnessed quite a few people pray with that same lack of confidence I displayed not so long ago. It's almost as if prayer has become a safety net for many rather than our first defense and our first impulse.

So how is God-crazy prayer different? God-crazy prayer rises up in us throughout the day, while we eat, think, walk, talk, worry, cry, laugh, seek fellowship, and run for solitude. Prayer without faith is stagnant, boring, and powerless, resulting in little to no fruit in our lives. God-crazy prayer is faith activating, engaging, and powerful—yielding fruit and a feeling of connectedness and intimacy with our Father.

While attending a Wednesday evening prayer service, I was blessed with the opportunity to witness both kinds of prayer in one setting: prayer that felt recited and uncertain and prayer filled with life and confidence. People were asked to stand up and share their requests out loud, and when they were finished, a few others in the circle would verbally commit to praying for those requests throughout the week. I listened to the simple requests as each person stood up to share. "Please pray for me. My car is having problems, and I really don't have the money for a new one." "Please pray for me. My job isn't going so well." All the requests were important, but the words of the prayer requests and the prayers that followed seemed to come out of hopelessness rather than hope. It wasn't the words being prayed that struck me, but the uncertainty with which they were prayed. People stated problems and troubles, and yet they seemed reluctant to call on God's power, strength, and promises. Even the room seemed to have a cloud of bleakness and doubt covering it.

That is, until the next prayer request.

A gentleman stood up to share how he was on the verge of suicide and struggling with severe depression. Dead silence hit the room as everyone sat there motionless, not quite sure how to respond. My hand shot up in the air, and I nudged my friend next to me so he would shoot his hand up as well. I wanted the leader to choose one of us to pray for this very serious request. I knew a prayer of faith and great authority must be prayed if this man was to see freedom from his situation. My friend was chosen to pray for the man, and as he began to pray with confidence and conviction, a new strength entered the room. Hope came over me as I listened to his prayer of faith. I didn't just notice the difference; I felt it in my spirit. Even the room seemed brighter and more joyful. I became excited about the act of prayer and the gift of praying for others. That night I recognized the first, halfhearted prayers as being very similar to my own in the past…and I recognized how stripping away concern for appearances or perfection releases the true power of prayer. Only when that man brought his despair to his Lord did the hope seem to cover us all. This is God-crazy prayer.

When you pray, do you feel your prayers are powerless or do you feel they are backed with confident faith? We must take prayer seriously if we are to see results. This can only take place when we are able to completely trust God and believe He has our best interest in focus, even when we don't understand, even when we can't see beyond our circumstances. Passionate, authentic prayer requires us to believe beyond what we see with the natural eye and reach for that which God has for us. We not only need to know who God is, but we must understand the power He has instilled in us, enabling us to live life in the victory He makes possible.

Cruising with the Captain

I never thought you would find me on a cruise. When I was pregnant with my sweet little Madison, I willingly went fishing out on the ocean near Destin, Florida. We had gone with some family and had the wonderful opportunity of learning the art of troll fishing. As you can imagine, I didn't do much fishing. Within a matter of seconds I was heading to the boat's tiny bathroom where I repeatedly got sick until we reached shore.

So when Disney cruises invited my family to come and see how a cruise really can be the most wonderful family vacation, I fought back my concerns about the open sea and accepted the amazing gift. I'm sure glad I did because it turned out to be one of our favorite family vacations.

When we entered the cruise ship, it became immediately apparent to me there was going to be a huge difference between my modest fishing boat experience and the big cruise ship experience. The ship was so large that I didn't even feel like I was on a boat. It was a relief to relax and let someone else tend to our every need for a change. The feeling of being able to go on a vacation and not worry about anything because every detail was taken care of was a blessing indeed. I never saw the captain, but I knew with all the confidence in the world that he had everything under control. I didn't have to see him or go to the captain's quarters or review his credentials to see how many ships he had captained. I could enjoy the cruise without all that. I simply trusted he would get the job done. Even if we were to run into choppy waters, I would be confident knowing the captain would handle the crisis. Of course, I would either have to trust him or jump ship, right?

What if you were on a weekend cruise to a destination you have always dreamed of when halfway into your trip you grow fearful and full of mistrust for the captain and the crew handling the ship? Your fear drives you to become irrational, and you begin to imagine the ship will be thrust into great danger. The more you dwell on it, the more you convince yourself it is going to happen. Your irrational thinking causes you to eventually barge into the captain's quarters attempting to take over the ship. People are trying to hold you back, but somehow you make your way past them and grab the ship's wheel from the captain's expert hands, only to realize you have no idea at all how to steer it, where to steer it, or even if you're supposed to steer it at all.

Sound far-fetched? Sound counterproductive? Sound ridiculous? You bet. It is as silly, useless, and absurd as not placing our trust in God, our heavenly Father and the Captain of our ultimate journey. How often do we try to grab the ship's wheel from our Captain and take matters into our own hands by not turning our prayers and praises over to Him?

Do we trust Him? Do we really believe in times of trouble, in time of financial crisis, in moments of difficult marital strife that God is who He says He is? We first must realize who has the control of our journey before we can have an intimate, confident, and powerful prayer life. Giving over control is not a one-time choice. It's a daily, moment-by-moment choice to believe God has our best interests in mind and that He loves us so much that He is interested in every detail of our lives. We have to learn to abandon ourselves in the same way we abandon land and our control when we get on a ship or a plane. We must leave our known life and completely trust that God will carry us to the next shore safely and for great purpose.

Even when we make a mistake and grab the wheel from our Captain and insist on taking the ship off its course, He will maneuver us back on track and into safe waters again. But this only happens if we will give Him control through prayer, submission, and trust. God will not force us to give up the wheel. We must do so willingly.

Whether we are on our road trip to God-crazy country or we are on a cruise far from our known life, the need for a Lord over our life is the same. Prayer not only keeps us afloat, it keeps us fearless for the most important journey of our life: our life!

Two-Ingredient Prayer

We can build up our trust in God when we examine the everyday things He does in our life. I don't mean that He has to pass our scrutiny as a reliable Captain. This examination is for us and our human need for proof. Even as a people of faith, we often turn back to the tangibles or clear bits of evidence. As we move toward God-crazy living, that need for proof gives way to peace and trust. But we are still on our way, and we are learning new faith skills with each stop along the trek. So for now, think on the many ways God has brought you through the fire and provided for your needs and heard your cries for help when faced with small and large troubles.

It's important to know He is in control and He will handle

every detail of our lives if we will relinquish them to Him. Prayer is a part of the relinquishment. We're saying, "Lord, I don't have the answers. I don't know what to do in this situation. Please help me." I have had to learn to say, "I don't know what to do." Is that as hard for you to say as it is—or at least was—for me? Who am I kidding? I still have times when I barely eke out expressions of my own inability and uncertainty. But when we speak of and confess our powerlessness, we are able to reach out to God for help.

Our prayers should be made up of two vital, God-crazy ingredients—sincerity and belief. Sincerity calls us to an authentic moment with God. Belief leads us through the prayer and into the time of waiting for and accepting an answer. If you start with sincerity and move forward in your prayer with belief, you will notice a greater capacity for discernment on your part and a more meaningful time of communion with Him.

Sincerity

When we strip away our personal pride and our desire to present perfection, we are left with a vulnerable, open heart. We need to be raw before the Lord. Even in our times of pure joy and praise, we must have a sincerity that comes from a very bare soul. Not barren, mind you, because we have great abundance in our spirits when we pray—but we must bare our souls. We must expose those flaws that we work so hard to hide from the rest of the world and even from ourselves. Think of Adam and Eve as an ideal example again. Before they pursued their own way and control, they had deep and secure communion with the Lord. Nothing came between them and their Creator. They were just as God intended His children to be with Him...open, willing, and filled with awe.

But as sin drifts into our lives and sifts down into our depths, the soul gets a bit cloudy, cluttered, and buried. Sincerity clears the way for true conversation with our Lord. We have nothing to hide behind or from when we start our prayers with a heart that is earnest and unaffected by our worldly desires or pursuits. Our lives are filled with distractions and details; some of which are important, others not so much. How do we go from the cluttered mind to the clean heart of sincerity? How do we go from our quest to be successful— if not perfect—to seeking the raw humility needed for prayer? Here are some ways that might help you come before the Lord with that spirit of sincerity. Keep in mind that these ideas are not necessarily for those moments of quick prayer when we are driving the car or waiting in line at the store. But as you foster your God-crazy, vibrant prayer life, these ideas might help you go deeper.

> *Building our faith...*
> *one experience after*
> *another is how we learn*
> *to engage our faith.*

CLEAR YOUR PHYSICAL SPACE

This isn't always possible, but it can be very helpful to either choose a simple, clean space in your home or to clear a space before going to the Lord. If you have found yourself distracted by dishes that need to be cleaned or work files that should be opened or emails that are still marked "unread," then shifting the place where you pray might help you shift how you pray. You will be more focused on who you are talking to during the prayer if you can ignore or look away from your main distractions for that time.

WRITE DOWN YOUR PRAYER NEEDS AND PRAISES

I get sidetracked. I love talking to God, but there are moments during prayer that my many tangents take me down rabbit trails of thought and emotion. Have you ever forgotten what you had wanted to tell God in the first place? If your days are so busy that you cannot bring your needs sincerely before Him, then keep a notebook to jot them down as they arise. By doing this, you will also become more connected to God during the day. When this becomes habit, you will be excited to add things to the list as you meet people with needs and prayer requests or as you relinquish your control bit by bit during the day. Your heart will become more prayerful and your life will become more prayer filled.

Ask Others for Prayer

Developing relationships which foster the sharing of prayer needs greatly blesses our lives. When we ask for prayer, we are reaching another level of vulnerability. What many don't realize is that this act of faith also builds our own prayer life. Why, you ask? Well, when we list our needs or praises to another and ask them to lift those up in prayer, there is a greater sense of accountability for us to do the same. For example, if you had a health concern and were telling everybody at church about it on Sunday and then calling your mentors and Bible study friends and other prayer warriors on Monday, and yet you didn't set aside time to bring it to God yourself, I'd be questioning your sincerity. Maybe you would do this because you give more weight to the prayers of others than to your own. But God wants you to bring everything to Him. If everyone on your prayer email distribution list is praying on your behalf, that is fabulous. But you also need to be speaking to God on your own.

Follow Through with Your Prayers

We will have many one-time prayers or one-of-a-kind requests to send up. We will also experience many of the same needs and concerns and trials over and over again. They might take different shapes, but chances are you have some regular worries or joys to talk over with God. If you are praying for healing or freedom from a sin or transformation in heart or even a more godly perspective about your job or spouse, then follow through with the prayers on a regular basis and also follow through with gratitude as God responds. Even when the answer is not yet clear, praise Him for hearing and loving you while you wait. Rejoice as prayers are answered.

Belief

Prayer must come out of our hearts, not our minds. The prayer itself, the recited prayer, is not what God is looking at. God knows our hearts and burdens before we even speak them. So why pray? It is the position of our hearts, the persistency in which we pray, and the belief that He is going to hear our prayer and act on our behalf that makes this part of the Christian life and the God-crazy life so active and alive.

There must be a belief in the Lord, a trust that He is in control, and a trust that He will do what He has promised. If we can trust the cruise ship captain to get us to the Bahamas, we can trust our heavenly Captain to steer us toward the desires of our hearts that come through Him. Building our faith one block at a time, one experience after another, is how we learn to engage our faith. It's how we commune with Him and learn who He is and what we mean to Him.

When I pray, I have realized that there is no need to go into every detail of my situation every time I pray. God knows what I'm dealing with and the burdens I carry. Instead, what I go into is either repentance or response. Repentance is needed when I have tried to turn the ship toward a new destination (which happens on occasion). Response is necessary because my reports help the Captain become aware of the crisis happening belowdecks. It's completely natural for my kids to come to me and report all of their problems, and believe me, they do. I cannot tell you how many prayers I have prayed just in response to what they have brought to me. Just as my children bring their requests to me because they know I will act on them, so we also must bring our requests and burdens before the Lord with faith, knowing He will work on our behalf.

Remember my example of the difference in prayers at the Wednesday night group? Some people prayed as though they were doubtful anything could be done with their situation. They sort of rattled off their problems like a grocery list, but they didn't actually bring those things to God. They either didn't feel the needs were significant enough or that they were not important enough to be heard by the Almighty. A God-crazy woman knows her place!

And it is kneeling before her God, who cherishes her, hears her, and longs for her to come to Him with absolute, unflinching, fearless, remarkable faith. The following parable from Scripture explains what it looks like to bring our petitions to the Lord with persistence, faithfulness, and hope.

> He told them a parable to the effect that they ought always to pray and not lose heart. He said, "In a certain city there was a judge who neither feared God nor respected man. And there was a widow in that city who kept coming to him and saying, 'Give me justice against my adversary.' For a while he refused, but afterward he said to himself, 'Though I neither fear God nor respect man, yet because this widow keeps bothering me, I will give her justice, so that she will not beat me down by her continual coming.'" And the Lord said, "Hear what the unrighteous judge says. And will not God give justice to his elect, who cry to him day and night? Will he delay long over them? I tell you, He will give justice to them speedily. Nevertheless, when the Son of Man comes, will he find faith on the earth?" (Luke 18:1-8).

This widow pressed in. She petitioned the judge over and over again, never giving up. Even when she heard the word no, she didn't lose heart. She was determined and passionate about gaining what she wanted from the judge. Jesus states clearly that He will not call the faithful to wait—but He does question whether He will find this kind of faith on the earth when He returns. So we cry out from the depth of our souls, we plead with Him day and night, and we press in with faith, knowing with certainty He will hear our cry and answer our request speedily.

❀ GOD-CRAZY MOMENT ❀

It's the little things that reveal to us just how much God truly cares about our lives. The year my son Aaron asked me if he could play football, I didn't really know what was required to get started. He was not forceful with his request, but he had a focused determination to make sure he got my attention and I was listening to him. I guess he knows his mama needs lots of reminding. He continued to mention it throughout the summer. It wasn't time for sign-ups, so I just tucked it away in the back of my mind, knowing I would handle it when the time came. Of course, the summer flew by and back-to-school preparations were in full force. Aaron was away at camp with the other kids, and I was left alone to myself for a few days.

While they were away, I'd been praying and asking the Lord to help me with this whole football thing. It sounds like such a simple thing, but to me it was a mystery. I've learned that when in doubt ask the Lord to bring me someone who can help, so for several days I was praying for this very thing.

When Saturday morning rolled around, I headed out for breakfast. This is one of my favorite rituals. I normally go to the same few places, but this day I decided to go to a little country diner some friends of mine own called the Henpeck Market. It is a quaint little country store off the beaten track and full of atmosphere. When I walked in the door, Don came over to say hello and quickly informed me that Jackie had left to get their son signed up for football since it was the last day to register, but she would be back any moment. My ears perked up. I enjoyed my breakfast and waited for Jackie to return so I could ask her my load of questions. She had answers to all of them, so I went straight from the restaurant to the field and signed Aaron up. I knew the Lord had orchestrated this opportunity for Aaron and for me. Because of the gift of that exact bit of information at the exact time, I didn't let Aaron down and God did not let me down. He revealed His mighty love for us both.

Just as Aaron kept reminding me of his passion for football, I was reminding God of what I would need as well. I wanted Aaron to be happy and to have this opportunity... I just needed a little help to make that happen. Correction: a lot of help. When we go to the Lord over and over to share our hearts—not merely repeating some list of what we want, but sharing our desires—He is pleased.

Over time you will have more special things only you and God may know about. There will be more and more treasures hidden deep down inside that rise up during your prayers. When those treasures reach Him, He holds them with care. He grants us the desires of our hearts according to His will. Our passions become His passions.

There are desires, treasures of the heart, that I have never shared with anyone, and they have come to pass in my life. God uses answered prayer to prove to me His faithful love. The small, intimate things that we give to Him and see come to pass are our reminders to trust Him in the more difficult times and for the bigger needs.

❧ La Vida Loca ❧

1. Do you feel connected to God when you pray? If not, have you ever felt a strong sense of God's presence? If you have felt it, when was that and what were you doing/living differently?

2. Have you engaged in the practices of a personal faith, such as prayer and meditation, or have these disciplines

fallen away? How do you hope to nurture these important parts of your faith life?

3. The Christian life is not worry free, but often we worry about something instead of praying about it. What are you fretting about that should be given over to God today?

4. Are you holding up your journey by interfering with the Captain? Do you question His ability and spend most of your days biting your nails with fear and questioning His truth?

5. What sins cloud your prayer time? Give them over to God with sincerity to experience a new level of prayer.

6. Do you ask others to pray for your needs? Do you pray for your own life decisions and needs?

7. Are you faithful when you tell others you will pray for them? If this has been hard for you in the past, make a commitment to follow through. You will notice such new depth in your connection to God when you are faithful with the petitions of others.

8. Can you prepare a quiet place for certain times of prayer? Set a goal to create a corner or an area in your home or maybe even outside that can be your more focused place of prayer. Determine what you will commit to this practice. Maybe you will pray there three times a week for ten minutes to start. Make a covenant with yourself and God to do this for one month.

9. Do you pray with belief? If you don't, there may be big and small hurts and disappointments from your past that keep you from full belief. Have God reveal them to you and have Him help you give them over to Him so that they do not cause you to stumble or hold back in your dialogue with Him.

10. What treasures have emerged from your heart during your times of prayer?

❧ GOD-CRAZY PRAYER ❧

Lord in heaven, I want to pray with conviction, belief, and trust. Give me a clean and pure heart for prayer. Challenge me to make a commitment to daily prayer for myself and others. I don't want to present my life to You with hopelessness and a fix-it attitude. I want to know that You hear me beyond a doubt. I want to lift up every prayer with a strong sense of Your power, might, and compassion. May I always be humble and sincere when I approach Your throne of righteousness. What joy I receive when I relinquish my idea of control or my misconceptions about how this journey should be. This is the surrendered faith I have longed for all of my days. I ask for it, and I shall receive. For You are good and loving and with me, Lord. Always. In Jesus' name. Amen.

13

PRAYING THROUGH THE TRIALS

Rejoice in hope, be patient in tribulation,
be constant in prayer.

ROMANS 12:12

When difficult times and bigger needs arise, is your first thought of those treasures we discussed earlier? Or does your mind surge with the power of the question, has my faith failed me? Or even the question, has God failed me?

On the cruise ship portion of our journey, where we are given the chance to experience faith as it can be when left to the control of our heart's Captain, we also can panic and experience waves of uncertainty that turn into tsunamis of doubt. Does that ring true in your life? When you get closer to authentic faith and all that this encompasses, do you also begin to question what you believe or how that belief should influence your life? This is usually when we look for ways to take matters into our own hands. We are afraid God is not doing His job. The God who has been faithful to us over the years suddenly seems silent or distant or occupied by the needs of others (there are a lot of people on this ship!). At least, this is what we convince ourselves is happening.

When a seeming crisis comes about, I have personally reached for that Captain's wheel a time or two. I have stubbornly looked at my life and determined that God either did not know what He was doing or He didn't fully understand what I needed. So I did it...I pushed open the door to the Captain's quarters (my heart), and I struggled to regain control of that wheel with gusto.

It was not pretty.

In fact, the storm grew darker and scarier, and the waves were swelling beneath me with such force that I could barely keep my feet on the floor, let alone my hands on the wheel. But I was determined to succeed because my belief was that if I could stand for even 15 minutes in the Captain's position at the helm and see the horizon, I would be able to make the right decisions for my life. I thought that by standing in that spot of control, I would have the same authority as God. That seems illogical, if not insane, but when the tough stuff happens it's easy to lose a bit of our commonsense faith.

Return to His Heart

Maybe I can save you a little heartache, friend. The thing about God-crazy women is that we can become passionate, quite passionate, about our lives and our purpose. That passion is meant to be for God's heart and His guidance for our lives, not in opposition to it. But sometimes we get ahead of ourselves. Are you with me on that?

When my faith fails me, my prayer may look something like this:

> Lord, please forgive me. Have mercy on Your daughter. I did not trust You. I did not have the faith to believe You would see my situation through. Now, because of my mistrust and my lack of faith, my situation is worse. Grant me mercy and help me in my situation. Give me wisdom. Give me guidance for the next steps of faith. I have made a complete mess of things, and now I need Your help more than ever to get me out of this situation. In Jesus' name. Amen.

I have some pretty clear memories of times when I have failed God and myself. Prayer is my way back to communion and relationship with Him. He does not distance Himself, but I had stepped away, and prayer always brings me back to the comfort of His mercy. And it's still there, even after we have tried to show off our life-control skills with disastrous results. Sometimes it's easier to trust God with the little things than the bigger things, and it's the bigger things that have the greatest consequence when we disobey or stray.

Repentance through prayer is a matter of the heart. God wants to know we are completely open to Him. We cannot be filled as we need to be unless our hearts are first emptied of our pride and arrogance. It's so important that we are completely remorseful when we realize our mistakes. This is not only about recognizing our own humanity, but acknowledging and

> *I believe that how we think of God...impacts the way we talk to Him.*

honoring God's divinity. We can only be remorseful if we understand the seriousness of our actions and the might of the God we serve.

A great life example of this is parenting. Kids are not going to be remorseful or regretful of things they do wrong unless they know the seriousness of what they have done. And even if their young minds don't comprehend the seriousness, they will understand it once they receive our response as parents. And we know the seriousness of their actions and our own because we have God's Word as our measure, and we have conviction of the Holy Spirit and our ongoing conversation with God through prayer.

The worldly standards of what is acceptable and what is not acceptable will never lead us to God's purpose. They will lead us to struggle for the control of that wheel. Until we take on the wisdom of Scripture and leading of the Lord to guide us and our passion for purpose, we will live a life of compromise, and believe me, we will live a life of many unnecessary storms and detours.

❈ GOD-CRAZY MOMENT ❈

When my grandmother was dying, the news was unexpected. We did not have the money available for me to fly to see her and join the family during this difficult time. We had just used our rainy day money right before. So we used the bill money, realizing that we needed God to provide. We needed to stretch beyond that desire to control everything and truly trust. I had confidence knowing I had done the right thing by going to be with my grandmother before she died. I didn't even know what a blessing it would be to my family that I chose to come until I was there with everyone. My sister and I were the only ones who could hold it together enough to plan the funeral and help with all the details. We were also the only ones who had the time to do so. We were given an opportunity to share the gospel and a time of worship as a testimony of my grandmother's life at her funeral. I was so grateful to be a part of all of it and to be with family, but when I returned home reality hit. I needed a financial miracle. So I prayed and asked God to respond in a big way! *Lord, You know my circumstances. You knew all of this was going to happen before any of it took place. I don't know what to do. I need You to intervene on my behalf. I need You to financially provide for the needs of our family, and I trust You completely, knowing You are fully in control of this ship. In Jesus' name. Amen.*

The Lord did provide and how He provided was completely unexpected. I knew exactly how much money I had in the bank. I also knew I had no money coming in over the next week. If I was going to get out of this situation, I would have to believe for a miracle. This does not mean pretending the situation does not exist. If we were

> on a ship and a storm was all around us, we would not sit there and deny the storm. We would believe God would pull us through the storm and that He would calm the waves to see us safely through the high seas.

It's not our job to figure out how God will do things. Our job is to press on and pray and to have belief for a miracle until an outcome is seen. I would rather die believing and trusting God with the results than die with unbelief and distrust in my heart. We must believe in God's control and the promises of His Word. If the things we hope for are not realized, then we must trust God with the outcome. When all is said and done, we did our part and can have confidence in knowing we did everything He requires of us.

We must not be afraid to ask for anything within God's will for us. When we fall to our knees before Him, our requests should not be about more than we need or about worldly success and affluence. We must always be asking ourselves where our treasure lies. If our treasure lies in kingdom things, then asking for earthly treasures of abundance counter that. I do not dwell on where I will live, how big my house will be, or what extras my car will have. If my car has problems, I think about what I need to do to get it fixed or to get a different car. If we'll eventually need a bigger house for our children, I wait to think about it until the need truly arises. God will show me what to do when those things become an issue. I'm not saying we have to live in poverty, but if our sights are set on excess or the levels of achievement we need to reach in order to feel good about ourselves and our lives, then we are poor, very poor, in spirit.

Different Ways to Pray

How do you pray? Most of us pray however we were taught to pray as kids or as new believers. That might mean lifting up concerns and praises in a conversational manner. Others might approach God with trepidation or fear and awe. I believe that how we think of God and how we know Him impacts the way we talk to Him. This isn't about right or wrong styles of prayer, but rather an exploration of ways to go deeper into the prayer waters. How can we become more intimate with God?

Communicative Prayer

Communicative prayer happens on a daily basis and is essential in the life of a believer. If we don't know the Father, then how can we really trust Him? I've heard people say that they don't pray for little things because God is so busy. Why would He take the time to answer our little ridiculous prayers? Again, remember, God looks at the heart. He looks at our faith, and it pleases Him greatly when we have a daily faith that draws us to His heart and His presence in all things. If we have faith for little things, this pleases God. He answers even the most insignificant prayers if they are within His will.

After a conference I was extremely late for my flight home. I had a very good reason for being late. I knew this particular conference was where I needed to be for kingdom purposes, and because of that I stayed as long as I needed to without worrying about the details of a missed flight. I didn't get anxious or upset; I knew God would take care of me. I was confident He would work it out for me to get home. I jumped into a cab after my meeting and began to pray: *Lord, You know I need to get home, and I need You to help expedite things at the airport so I can make this flight. I need Your help in this situation, Lord. Please help me get the flight and get home.*

I'm not always into praying such specific prayers, but I was communicating from my heart, talking with the Lord and listening quietly to His direction. As I rushed from the cab into the airport, I looked over at the ticket counter and saw a long line wrapped around several posts, and my first thought was, *How in the world will I ever make this flight?* Yet I knew from past experience that it was all in God's hands. I immediately whispered under my breath, "I trust

You, Lord." Out of nowhere this gentleman in uniform approached me and asked if I needed help. Now remember, I am in an airport full of people, and the chances of this guy choosing me to walk up to were slim to none—in human chances, that is.

"Yes!" I quickly replied. "I need to get on a flight in thirty minutes and I have bags to check." He grabbed my bags, walked me over to the first-class counter, placed my bags on the baggage carrier, and handed my itinerary to the ticket agent. Within just a few minutes, and without me having to say another word, they were handing me my boarding pass. Even though I had prayed, I was shocked. Airports seem to be one of the places God has chosen to do miracles in my life. Or should I say airports seem to be the place where I have needed and trusted God to do miracles in my life?

Communicative prayer is all about talking to God while going through the process of our daily life. It is our way to commune with Him and ask Him for wisdom every step along the way. We place trust in Him knowing He will be there for us when we need Him. These ongoing conversations with God help us to draw close to Him and to feel a stronger connection with Him so that when the heavier stuff comes along, we know what He is able to do.

Contemplative Prayer

Another form of prayer essential in the life of a believer is meditative and reflective in nature. Personally, being quiet takes a minor miracle…at least that used to be the case. But as I have matured in my walk and with my prayer practices, I can enjoy quiet times before the Lord. Admittedly, it has taken years for me to fully understood the value of contemplative prayer and even longer to embrace how to actually do it. This type of prayer is more planned and intentional; therefore, with a big family and all of my other responsibilities it's difficult for me to work this style of prayer into my life. You may know just what I'm talking about! Perhaps you've considered how meaningful and spiritual contemplative prayer could be, but then you've examined your life, just as I have, and thought, *Maybe not.*

I actually have to schedule time alone with God to be able to participate in contemplative prayer.

The word "meditative" can seem scary for some Christians because the New Age movement and other Eastern religions use this term in their lingo, but they use meditation for different reasons. Christian meditation is focused on Jesus and His teachings, not on self. The meditation or contemplative prayer I am speaking of has everything to do with Jesus and God's Word. "Contemplative" simply means "deep in thought, meditative, pensive, and reflective." The word "meditative" has more than one meaning, but the definition I am speaking of is "pondering something, the act of thinking about something deeply and carefully." In *The Pleasures of God,* John Piper writes, "When I preached on the pleasures of God back in 1987, I jotted down in my notes one Sunday this summary aim and prayer:

> Portray his pleasures in preaching.
>
> Behold his glory in listening.
>
> Approach his likeness in meditation.
>
> Display his worth in the world."

When we meditate on God's Word, He reveals Himself to us in a deeper way that helps us in our approach to be more like Him. God's Word can be used in this form of prayer and brings about healing, relaxation, and peace in our lives. This can be done by listening to an audio CD of Scripture or simply by writing out a passage of Scripture you would like to think on. I use this type of prayer time to ask the Lord to help me become aware of areas in my life that need to be transformed and areas in my life that are sinful or based on any deceptions. I also use this type of prayer to strengthen my spirit when I am feeling weak.

At this point in my life this type of prayer is necessary simply in order to survive where I am in my Christian journey. These moments might happen when I am on a plane for two hours and am just sitting there studying the Word, when I am in my car for long periods of time, or when I am alone at home. Or they can be more obvious moments, such as on a retreat in the quietness of the country. Where are you in your journey? Do you long for times of peace, for moments when you can sit and listen to something God might be trying to say? I encourage you to seek opportunities for this kind of communication with God. This type of prayer rejuvenates the spirit and gives life to our journey.

Intercessory Prayer

You will know when you need to pray and fight the battle for yourself or for others. You will understand when you need to be persistent and faithful as you call out to God to hear your cries, your pleas, and your heart.

Are you in a marriage where all hope is lost? Have your children walked away from the Lord? Do you have unsaved loved ones? Are you fighting depression? Have you been abused and cannot get beyond the pain? There are also times when we need others to battle in prayer with us. I have been in situations where I was too weak to pray and feeling too discouraged to have faith. In this case call the prayer warriors you know and ask them to pray for you. These are usually people close to you who will have a burden for your circumstances and really intercede on your behalf.

What about the times when you don't really know how or what to pray? This is when the Holy Spirit prays through you for someone else. Romans 8:26-27 says, "The Spirit helps us in our weakness. For we do not know what to pray for as we ought, but the Spirit himself intercedes for us with groanings too deep for words. And he who searches hearts knows what is the mind of the Spirit, because the Spirit intercedes for the saints according to the will of God."

If you have accepted Christ, then you have the Holy Spirit living in you. He is the Comforter (John 14:16 KJV). There have been many times when I have just been going along in my day and the Holy Spirit has placed someone on my heart. I immediately pray for that person. Not knowing exactly what to pray for, I ask the Holy Spirit to guide my words and give me wisdom on how to pray. My faith alone is what God desires to see, and me standing with my brother or sister in Christ is what's most important.

Warfare Prayer

I have left the most essential form of prayer in the Christian journey for last. The terms spiritual warfare might be foreign to you, scary to you, or not for you at all, but I want to emphasize that this type of prayer is essential in the life of every believer and not meant for only some. Forget the terminology for a moment. Let's just go to Scripture as a source for what I am trying to communicate. Most people I have met over the years seem to leave this type of prayer for more mature believers, thinking serious prayer comes later in our walk with Christ. Quite the contrary is true. It is important to learn this type of prayer early on as young believers.

> For many of us, prayer can be a last resort.

It's easy to move along in our Christian journey unaware of the enemy's tactics, but when we find ourselves in the midst of that spiritual battle, we can rely only on what we know because we have no time to learn anything new. We are in the thick of our circumstances, and all around us are distractions that occupy our thoughts, prayers, worries, and time as we try to wade through the trials and difficulties we may be facing. Again, I want to stress the importance of keeping our eyes on our Captain, not on the distractions, the trials we are facing, or the disappointments we are enduring. We really have no reason not to be prepared if we are following God and His Word. He has given us all the ammunition we need to fight the battles we face in life. We are not to be so immersed in our lives, our wants, and our daily living that we forget who we are living for and the power He gives us to counter every battle.

One of my friend's sons joined the Marines. They trained him thoroughly in the area of weapons and made sure he understood the tactics our enemies have used in the past. They even put him in situations where he could experience types of warfare our enemies use when in battle to prepare him should he ever have to face similar circumstances while at war. Our military doesn't wait long before exposing soldiers to the more serious issues the military deals with. No, they throw them into a simulation of a battle's sounds, dangers, traps, strategies, and pressures. I was amazed at what these young boys go through. I think they are somewhat unaware of what lies ahead for them at boot camp and combat training until they actually experience it themselves. In our walk with God, we also don't know what lies ahead for us.

In George Barna's book *The Revolution,* he exclaims, "Is society dragging you in the opposite direction from where Jesus calls you? Then acknowledge that your life is part of a spiritual war between God and Satan, declare your side, and get on with it. Admit that you are better off 'fighting the good fight' and suffering on earth for the cause of Christ than winning the world but losing your soul for the balance of eternity. Get used to life in the context of warfare. Every breath you take is an act of war. To survive in the midst of the spiritual battle in which you live, seek a faith context that will enhance your capacity to be Christlike."

So what does prayer in battle look like? The heart must be determined to persevere no matter what. This in itself is a challenge for us today because we've been spoiled by overnight deliveries, fast food on every corner, information at our fingertips via the Internet, and all the other conveniences we have grown to depend on. It isn't easy to think of laboring over anything or being patient for an answer.

For many of us, prayer can be a last resort. Trials come, the problems begin, and we run straight for our worldly comforts instead of the prayer closet. We run to food, sex, shopping, alcohol, or other forms of medicating. We get on the phone and tell a dozen of our friends the problem. The point is not so much what we run to, but that we run toward things other than God. Only after discovering that nothing else works do we find ourselves on our faces before God, begging Him to intervene. The importance of communicative prayer comes into play here. If we are communing with God throughout our days, then it will be our natural inclination to seek Him when we sense a battle coming on and before, when we are unaware of what is going to happen. If we are steadfast in our walk, in our prayer life, and in our pursuit of God, we will be equipped to use His instruction when battle begins. We will be mentally, emotionally, and physically prepared to persevere. We will press in and not give up.

When the battles begin, what do you run to sometimes instead of God? Whatever you list as your response is most likely a part of the battle. Anything that we choose as our first line of defense over faith becomes an obstacle to our faith and our protection. Understand that the struggles you experience are a very real part of the battle. We will one day graduate before our King as a spiritual being, and we will reign in glory with Him forever, but unlike the United States Marines, we do not have to earn the right to do so. When we said yes to our awesome wonderful Savior, when we invited Him to live in our hearts to reign over our lives, we were made daughters and sons. Our names are now written in the book of life, and we are extended grace and mercy for our sins, but while on this earth we are in a daily battle against the enemy who wars for our souls and against our flesh, which finds ways to entice and captivate us, keeping us distracted from living the life of freedom God offers. How do we do battle with the enemy, and how do we overcome in the dark trials of our lives? We embrace the position of a God-crazy woman and know our source is God Himself. I know you can do it.

Prayer is crucial in our lives. It is our connection to God in addition to His Word.

☘ La Vida Loca ☘

1. Ask yourself if you really trust God:
   - With your life
   - With your kids
   - With your husband
   - With your finances
   - With your future
   - With your dreams
   - With your heart
   - With your trials

2. Remember to repent when you take matters into your own hands as a result of your unbelief.

3. Ask yourself, why pray if you don't believe God can answer your prayers?

4. Ask God to help you trust Him completely so you can give yourself to Him with abandon.

5. Think on the times when God has pursued you.

6. Journal God-crazy moments when you had answers to prayer. Read these when you are waiting on God for an answer to prayer so that you will be encouraged in your faith. The Israelites would forget over and over again what God had done for them and would be misled or disobey as a result.

7. Take a couple of weeks and think about incorporating these different ways of praying into your life: communicative, contemplative, intercessory, and warfare prayer.

8. Remember that faith is believing beyond your circumstances. What current situations do you need to believe beyond?

9. When did you last pray for a specific situation and for a specific result? Were you uncomfortable doing this? Were you able to pray with belief? Now, our answer might not be what we want it to be when we do this, but it is very important to understand our heart at the time. Are we able to pray with confidence in the Lord?

10. List those things or people or beliefs you sometimes run to instead of God when you sense a battle is taking place. Pray about these and ask God to guard your heart and redirect your heart to Him each time.

❧ GOD-CRAZY PRAYER ❧

Lord, help me to give up control of my life to You. Help me abandon myself so that I may draw closer to You. Help me to place my complete trust in You and not be distracted by the circumstances around me. Lord, help my faith not to fail me when the trials come, and when darkness closes in around me. Help me to remain steadfast with determination and complete faith that You will see me through. In Jesus' name. Amen.

An Ordinary Life Exchanged for the God-Crazy Life

I've walked these streets barren, with nothing left to glean,
Traveled far to other lands and in the people I have seen,
Hopelessness and sorrow behind hollow eyes I met,
Brokenness and pain from all secrets kept.

I've sat with kings, dined with the rich. They told me of their lives,
We laughed, we danced together and no tears were cried,
Walls and layers of castles were not as strong indeed,
As those kept around their hearts so all remained unseen.

Though rich, their eyes empty, paupers but not known,
Pain and sorrow seen behind laughter they had shown.
The dance was not a dance of joy but one missing in step,
And in darkest chambers were found tears quietly wept.

The cries pierce my heart; sadness moves my soul,
Redeemed at last, forgiven, finally made whole,
I long to see this beauty unfold before my eyes,
My children freed from chains that bind, now be satisfied.

I must give my life, exchange it for all lost,
The Lamb slain for burdened sin the ultimate cost,
All taken on Calvary so suffering will be no more,
This crown of thorns above my brow releases prison doors!

The lame shall walk, the blind shall see,
Secret shame and failure given up to me,
All stolen and destroyed restored to those who mourn,
Joy, hope, peace, and love to them must now adorn.

No longer an ordinary life for those who give all,
But one set high above soaring toward the call,
When they dance they dance with delight knowing they are free,
To love and serve their master, who loves them lavishly!

—*Michelle*

14

GOD-CRAZY LIVING

*A "God-crazy" person is tired of striving to
live an "ordinary" life, a powerless life, a life filled with
to-do lists hoping somehow obligation alone will make
them a better Christian, and instead chooses to live an
adventurous Christian life, a life of purpose instead of
perfection, and a life that has meaning.*

—MICHELLE BORQUEZ

During a very difficult time I spent a dark night praying, asking God for the plan for my life. I felt afraid and alone, and I was starting to believe the litany of self-doubt that had been running through my mind for much of that year. In the silence of the night and the loneliness of the moment, I was flooded by my worries related to taking care of my family, my work, my future. In fact, I think my list of worries was so long I didn't even get to the future concerns. I couldn't embrace hope for the next day, let alone hope for many tomorrows later.

Sooner or later we all want a plan, a list of things to do, and a strategy to tackle that list of things to do. Whether we are perfectionists or unorganized women, most of us hit a point when we want a plan that is clearly before us. And we want a plan that suits our desires and our version of a vision. This motivates us to start writing out our own plans and our next steps.

But before we reach for our calendars and our spreadsheets to map out a life, we need to see planning for what it is—our mechanism to avoid having to place our faith and trust in God. This is big, my friend. I'm not advocating winging it and not taking responsibility, or not being wise with money and resources because God's got your back. Faith-filled living doesn't mean we relinquish our God-given responsibilities such as stewardship, wisdom, and decision making bathed in prayer. But you don't have to have it all figured out. Most of the time women want the security of a plan, and we need this security to be our very best...we just have been misplacing our faith when it comes to who should be making that plan!

In that time of doubt and frantic fretting about what would happen to me and my family, God conveyed to me a truth I had never before recognized. "Michelle, I am the plan." There is no perfect plan outside of God and His wisdom. The turmoil inside my heart subsided as I felt Him comfort me. "You don't need to worry. You don't need to strive. I will take care of you. I will be your husband, your lover, your guide, and your protector." I have to admit it took me a few years to really believe God meant what He said to me, but I can say wholeheartedly that He has been all those things to me and more.

God-crazy living requires us to throw out our plan and let God *be* the plan.

What if We Break Down?

We have a very capable Driver for our road trip—I think we are in agreement about that. So far, even with the bumps and a few detours, the trip has been good and we've witnessed God's faithfulness. But tell me something. As you watch the days go by and your excitement builds and wanes, depending on the particular stretch of the road, do you start to wonder what would happen if you broke down or ended up in the ditch with pieces of your life strewn about the road? Doesn't the very thought of that make you want to 1) panic, 2) take charge again, and/or 3) sign up for roadside assistance coverage with every provider you can think of?

Because trouble and pain have been a part of our lives, we have programmed ourselves to think we need to be in control at all times. We have told ourselves that heartache and trials will be warded off if we just have a more solid plan and if we protect that plan at all costs. We know from experience that we can feel confident, strong, and resilient at one stop along our way and then face a sharp, sudden curve that leaves us stranded, vulnerable, and helpless. How many

> *God isn't meant to be our form of emergency roadside assistance.*

times have you stood on the narrow shoulder of that life freeway clutching your belongings, your heart, and your hopes, looking to the left and then to the right at seemingly endless blacktop and yellow stripes without seeing any sign of help on the way? I was in that very place that night I was praying for a plan and for God to save me from my situation.

Life does not come with catastrophic insurance. And when we choose to be in charge of our own plan—or our own vehicle through this journey—we will end up stranded, not by God, but by our powerlessness. In my situation, I hadn't been taking my life plan and purpose through regular maintenance checks with God. I'd been shining up the chrome and retouching the paint job, and I had polished the mirrors to all look good on the outside so others would not suspect that any part of me was broken, but I had neglected the internal workings that made life run smoothly in the direction of my God-given purpose.

Fear of the unknown keeps us from all God has for us when it comes to spiritual adventure. Somehow we think it's easier to follow a list of rules or to keep up appearances while letting our spiritual lives deteriorate. This keeps us from having to believe and trust in God for our lives. If we just stick to the dos and don'ts we think we are okay in our Christianity; we're "good enough." Yet that life does not lead to godliness, and it certainly isn't on the God-crazy map. It isn't until we are in the driver's seat moving along on our safe little road trip, where we have planned every element of the trip out in order to keep any disasters from happening and no surprises from appearing that we suddenly hit a road bump and find ourselves thrown out the window and onto the pavement, asking ourselves questions like: "Lord, I had my seat belt on, so why did You let this happen to me? I had everything planned out. I followed all the rules. And yet here I am sprawled out like a fool for everyone to see me, and where are You in all of this?"

I hope that many of us will hit the God-crazy road to surrender before we find ourselves in a wreck, but most of us need trials to perfect us, grow us, and force us to look at ourselves and go deeper. Some of us get to the point where black smoke is billowing out of our vehicle, and we no longer can hide the fact that we are not moving. We can be mid-breakdown on that freeway, and still thinking we might be the one to save ourselves—or better yet, maybe our salvation will come in the form of a certain job or a man or the approval of someone we failed in the past.

If we jump in the car with God, you'd better believe He is going to make sure the car is a well-oiled machine that can transport us to new venues. He will replace loose sparkplugs, get those fluids flushed and refilled, and select the best tires the industry has to offer. But God isn't meant to be our form of emergency roadside assistance. He is meant to be with us every mile of the journey. When this is true for our lives and we do end up with pieces of our heart or our big plans scattered behind us, He is right there. He never abandons us. And the best part of all…He knows exactly where we are supposed to be going next.

✾ GOD-CRAZY MOMENT ✾

We look for answers in creation rather than the Creator. I met a young woman recently while having breakfast at my favorite bagel place. She was so beautiful, and she had the most adorable hat on. It isn't often you see women braving a hat, so I complimented her style. We immediately struck up a conversation (you know how us girls can go on) and began finding things we had in common. There are not too many moments where I feel God prompt me to share about Christ in a bolder way, but this was one of those occasions. While she was talking I thought of ways to bring up the subject. She began sharing her philosophies, and I could tell that she had bought into the whole idea of becoming a powerful woman of success. So I said to her, "How do you attempt to become a woman of success, a woman of influence and power?" She responded passionately and without hesitation with the idea of her possessing all it takes to do so. She really felt confident the power was within herself and she began to share with me her pursuit of Buddhism. My heart sank a little, but it only caused me to be more determined to not let her walk away without sharing Christ with her. So I said to her, "When you trust in yourself, when you depend on your own abilities, you limit yourself to what power and influence you have in this world. There is a greater power, a greater way to live your life, and that is through the salvation of Christ Jesus." I went on to explain to her how we are limited in our minds to what we know. We don't know the future, and ultimately we have no control over what our life will look like, but if we put our faith in God, His power will live in us, and His power is so much greater than our own.

We talked in length and spent the better part of the day together. She was so open to what I shared with her. I realized she was seeking truth. I told her to pray and ask God to reveal truth to her. Truth is the only thing God can use to set us free from the deception and lies of the enemy.

The God-Crazy Exchange

Have you ever been to a street fair or the rows and rows of stalls at a Mexican marketplace? There are so many wonderful, colorful items to choose from. And once the choice is made, that is when the bartering begins. It isn't always a natural thing to do, and to some, bartering feels like you are trying to be cheap. But a very interesting, telling aspect of negotiating a price for a desired item is that we must first think through how much we value both the money in our pocket and that tempting item we either desperately want or need. We don't merely read a price tag and hand over the cash.

Okay, you are probably thinking, *Why on earth is she bringing up shopping when we are working so hard to not cling to materialism in our journey toward God-crazy freedom?* I'm not changing the subject. Not really. Because when we reach for that wonderful, colorful God-crazy life, we are offering something in exchange for that quest of faith. Bartering is a great example because many of us want to negotiate what we offer in exchange because the price is often higher than we wanted to pay. But what we don't realize is that the value of what we are getting is so beyond what we sacrifice. Each of us will bring forth something different from our lives as an offering...but it will be the same currency. We give up world-crazy living in order to receive the God-crazy abundant life.

Giving up the world doesn't mean we can't have fun or go to the movies or laugh or ever shop again. It doesn't mean we have to put up our house for sale and give away our entire DVD collection (though you will probably get pickier about what you buy), nor does God crazy require us to disown all ties to the world; we do still have to function here. It does mean that your desires can and will change, and that you might be asked to let go of something or even someone at a point along the way. You might have to release your hold on a specific dream. But the exchange is well worth it. When you extend your broken offering with trembling hands, you will engage in transformation. This is a something for nothing trade... as in there is *nothing* that compares to this new life of abundance, wholeness, and perfection we are given. Look at all that we receive and what happens when you let go of your world-crazy holdings and embrace the adventure:

1. Pure joy each time you surrender something new to God's heart.

2. A faith that permeates your being so much that it is your primary influence, and it will draw people to you and to God.

3. God's passionate pursuit of you will ignite your desire to pursue all He is.

4. You'll make decisions with the intention of pleasing God first.

5. Faith obedience gives you a life of peace even in the midst of chaos.

6. You will speak the language of love with conviction and compassion.

7. The combination of a queenly spirit and a servant's heart breathe new confidence and meaning into your purpose.

8. Your old agendas for relationships fade as God's new agenda restores and rejuvenates relationships with family, friends, coworkers, and others.

9. God-crazy women know themselves as the beautiful handiwork of God, and they see such beauty in others.

10. You cherish your identity as a work in progress because it means you are never stuck but are always growing.

11. You relinquish the burden to be perfect and embrace God's desire to be shown perfect in you through the Holy Spirit.

12. You won't need to wonder where you are going because God will show you what step to take next.

God says to us, "I love those who love me, and those who seek me diligently find me" (Proverbs 8:17). When we seek Him we will hear His voice, we will feel His leading, and we will know the ways in which we should go. God-crazy living yields prosperity on every level, spiritual, physical, and emotional health. World-crazy yields us emptiness, depression, addiction, bondage, loneliness, anger, and bitterness. Need I go on?

Examples from women's lives are some of the most influential resources available to us. We are going to be looking at God-crazy lived out to the fullest, not just in God-crazy moments, but in life-long commitments to pursuing God, thriving in His pursuit, and shining in His power. Seeing authentic faith lived out helps us understand our own maps toward adventure. When God calls us to new directions, we can rest in knowing that others are on this journey as well, and they are faithful and all-out God crazy. Join on in.

❧ LA VIDA LOCA ❧

1. Did you ever have a dark night? Was it brought on by a desire for a plan from God or from a failed plan of your own? What brought you to your knees that time?

2. Are you a planner? What will be the hardest part of giving your future over to God?

3. How have you been left without security in your life? Did a parent or a friend or a spouse leave you feeling abandoned? Do you hold on to that as an example of what happens when you trust? Pray to be released from that pain and pray to give these times over to God.

4. If you just *have to* keep planning, maybe you could start plotting out how you will let God *be* the plan in

your life. What will you do differently? How will this look different?

5. When have you broken down? Was there a major crash or have you had quite a few "incidents." Does anyone notice, or do you cover up these times quickly so that nobody knows that you are not in control.

6. When you think of the unknown, what rises up? Worry? Fear? Terror? A whole list of past hurts? What is the worst case scenario that you can think of...if you turned over your unknowns to God? Say it out loud, pray it, and also let this go.

7. How have you settled for "good enough" instead of going God crazy in the past? How are you tempted to do the very same even now?

8. Do you blame God for your wrong turns?

9. Are you holding back from surrender or are you all-out God crazy?

10. What value do you place on your current way of living? What value do you place on the new, joyful, surrendered life God has for you? Are you ready for the exchange?

⚜ GOD-CRAZY PRAYER ⚜

Lord, I am so ready for God-crazy living. Your pursuit of me still amazes me, and I pray that it does all the days of my life. What a gift to be loved unconditionally, even when I have stood knee-deep in the wreckage of my own making. Now I understand that the love I have looked for in others and in the world's offerings has been waiting for me all along in Your arms. I'm so ready to trade the bits and pieces of effort and self and mistakes for Your treasures. When I said yes to this adventure, I didn't know what surrender looked like, I only knew that I was tired of pretending to be in control. Now I see the beauty of the transformed life within reach…it is at the end of my hands when they are outstretched toward You. Thank You, Lord, even for the uncertainties in my life. They draw me closer to Your perfection and Your unconditional acceptance. In Jesus' name. Amen.

15

A NEW WAY TO WORSHIP

Worship in the Son
Worshipping you takes me to another place,
Where mountains are not quite so hard to climb,
Suddenly I'm no longer in the race,
And you become much easier to find,

Every tear I cry is one that moves you,
And I find joy in knowing you are there,
Looking at my heart you see right through me,
All my faults lay out before you leave me bare,

And yet I find myself just walking in the Son,
With your rays of light embracing me again,
Walking down this road of life as one,
Knowing you will always have my hand.

—MICHELLE

Church happened in my home every day. Mom would pull out her guitar in the evening and we would worship, or we would have friends over for fellowship and prayer. Our life was filled with constant activity and attitude that led us back to faith as our foundation. While I grew up with so much biblical life being acted out before me daily, it wasn't until these past few years I realized the treasure given to me in my youth. This daily expression of my faith is where the passion lies; it's where the excitement is. Being a part of the church—the body of Christ—on a daily basis keeps me alive in my Christianity. Seeking opportunity to gather with like-minded and like-hearted friends for prayer and fellowship, seeking to worship in moments of quietness, allowing church to happen in the most unique places is how I have learned to look at my life, and it's what has brought me to the place of living a God-crazy life.

Worship is so much more than just a few praise songs at church. Worship is so much greater when we come broken before Him, hearts bowed, with the understanding of who we are worshipping. Broken people, hungry for God, desperate for Him to restore our lives to wholeness, is one way we approach worship; but there are other times when worship is purely an expression of our love for God. Worship takes on a whole new meaning when we come broken before Him. Ultimately the things that break each one of us and humble us are different. What humbles me is not going to necessarily humble you, but God knows the things He needs to allow to happen to grow us and bring us to our knees, to the place where we worship Him out of our gratefulness for His faithfulness.

My faith-changing brokenness happened unexpectedly. I thought I was broken before, and in many ways I had been, but brokenness and the struggles that form a contrite heart are an ongoing process in life. We are never broken enough in one instance to experience the full magnitude of the cross in our lives. It's an ongoing process of being broken over and over again. I said I would never be divorced. I said I would never walk away from God. I felt strong in my faith and loved the Lord with all my heart. I recited many things to myself that I would never do, and yet I did them, and even thought things I never deemed possible. When trials came, I even walked away from Him in my heart. But God brought me to a place where He would shine His light on my humanity in a way that was very uncomfortable but transforming.

I'm describing this time in my life to give you support in your own difficulties and weaknesses. I cannot bring you enough comfort to make you *comfortable* in those circumstances because through your discomfort you will seek God as Provider and Redeemer. In your failures God reveals Himself to you in ways you never dreamed.

We live in a broken world, where circumstances can rip apart our lives, and worship plays a big part in healing the brokenness of our hearts. Worship heals the wounded places. It allows forgiveness to flow, anger to disappear, and as my poem expresses, worship takes us out of the race—the everyday feeling of striving to be better, striving to be enough, striving to hold it together—and brings tremendous peace. It's here, in the sanctuary of our worship (wherever the worship actually takes place), that we are able to overcome and find freedom from the things binding our lives. It's here that we are able to find peace to manage a way, God's way, through the muck of it all. Worship ignites my heart with mercy, grace, compassion, and immense love.

Worship is the sanctuary God has created for us to be washed clean, to be healed, and to be set free. While in the act of worship, in the spiritual place of worship, and in the mind-set of worship, we find our audience of One…God. I remember one evening I was in my living room alone, playing my keyboard and worshipping the Lord. I had always imagined God would use my gift of music to touch the lives of others, and up to this point He had not done so in the way I had expected. I thought I would lead worship in church, or maybe one day even do a worship CD, but this was not how my life unfolded. In fact, music was the only gift God had chosen not to fully use in my life.

This one particular night I stood playing my keyboard and singing out worship songs to Him as I had done many nights before. I began to worship Him and was swept away by His presence. As I shared my heart with the Lord, telling Him how sorry I was not to have ever used my gifting of music and song for Him in the way I had planned, in the midst of my singing and worshipping Him, God softly whispered to me a profound truth I had never recognized. "Michelle, you were created to worship Me not for others, but for Me alone. When you worship, it is not to touch someone else's life, but it is so that you might be touched by My presence." I suddenly got it. My gifts were not created for me or for anyone else; they were created and given to me by a holy God who desires for me to bring my gifting to Him as an offering of worship. Oh, how I want people to have a relationship with my audience of One. How I want everyone with hidden or celebrated gifts to know just how those gifts were meant to be used.

From that day forward worship for me has never been the same. I finally understood the meaning behind worship. Worship is a position of the heart in everything we do. When I am serving my brother, I am worshipping God; when I am feeding the poor, I am worshipping God. For worship is to bring everything I am before Him as an offering. It's offering up my life to be used in any way He sees to use it. When I worship Him, whether it is alone in my living room or before people, I am worshipping and praising my audience of One. Worship is an expression of my love for Him.

When our bodies are extremely thirsty or hungry, the desire for sustenance is so strong we almost feel that if we don't satisfy this need we will pass out from the lack. Spiritually we are the same. When we are empty inside, when we feel parched and ravenous, we search for fulfillment and often we look for it in the counterfeit offerings of the world. What we must know is the only thing that will quench our soul's thirst is God. One of my favorite worship songs is called "Hunger." It resonates with me because it is all about our need for Christ, whose love never runs empty.

God-Crazy Worship: Diana's Story

When I saw Diana for the first time, she was up on stage leading worship at church. I have seen a lot of people lead worship over the years, but something was different about Diana. I could tell worship was an extension of her heart. Her countenance, her energy with which she worshipped, and the way she seemed almost detached from the world around her, were clear indications to me of a deeper walk. As I grew to know Diana over the past few years, my assumptions were proven right as I found her to be a person of great depth.

Diana and I met at my favorite little bagel shop in town. Actually, it might not have been the best of ideas to try to do an interview about worship while at the same time trying to eat a yummy chewy bagel. Thankfully, the two of us are pretty good at multitasking and able to eat and talk at the same time. While we were in the middle of the interview, Diana eagerly shared with me her view on worship summed up in an exhilarating quote from William Temple about worship: "It is the submission of all our nature to God. It is the quickening of our conscience by His holiness; the nourishment of mind with His truth; the purifying of imagination by His beauty; the opening of the heart to His love; the surrender of will to His purpose, and all this is gathered up in adoration, the most selfless emotion of which our nature is capable and therefore the chief remedy for that self-centeredness which is our original sin and the source of all actual sin."

> *I thought,*
> THIS IS DEEPER;
> THIS IS REAL.
> —*Diana*

Diana has been involved with music most of her life. She has a real passion to lead worship and currently leads worship at the church she attends. Diana is also the director of a preschool she started this past year in order to reach out to Hispanic and lower income families. In addition to all of these acts of service and ministry, she nurtures and cares for her husband and two children. The following is Diana's insightful story conveyed during an interview I did with her. I pray that it offers you the inspiration and power that it did for me.

DIANA, HOW DID YOU EVENTUALLY EMBRACE THE ACT OF WORSHIP?

Back in 1980, when I became a Christian, I never really heard people talking about worship much. I was saved through a campus ministry at my college, and because I knew how to play guitar and sing, I was asked to lead music a lot. I later became the music leader at Campus Crusade for Christ. They didn't call me the "worship leader," but we'd sing worship songs, going from one song to the next, and they had meaning, and they were moving, but I personally didn't know what the meaning of worship was at the time.

It wasn't until about four years later when I moved to Boston and began participating on the worship team at a little Baptist church when the full meaning of worship became real in my life for the first time. Now when I sang, it was all about expressing adoration for God. I began to experience something very different...something I had never experienced in the church up until this point. Each time I would lead worship I would focus on coming to God's throne in adoration. Part of the reason for this transformation in my life was simply because the leadership of the church demonstrated in such an obvious way this vertical communication with God. Again, this was something I had never seen before. They would address the congregants openly, in a very real and authentic way, talking to God collectively as if He were immediately before us instead of far away. During worship we would sing the songs, but we would also savor the songs and take time to listen and wait on the Lord.

When I began to experience this amazing newfound presence of worship in my life, I thought, *This is deeper; this is real.* It was truly life changing for me as a worship leader, but even more so as a child of God. I had been in this desert, this season of drought in my life. I might even describe it as a breaking away from God. Now here I was experiencing Him in a new way, a very real way. He brought me back to Himself and into His fullness. God used music to draw me to Himself, but my experience in worship was still limited to the music time at church and had not yet spilled over to my daily walk. I started leading worship more and more, and was being discipled by the worship leaders, not in a formal sense, but just by being with them and learning from them. They took the time to mentor me and demonstrated a very real relationship with God.

I began to experience so much more of God in every area of my life. Worship became a call to my heart and a reminder of God's attributes. I realized why I was singing and worshipping. It was truly an intimate expression of my love for God. Those years in my life were huge in terms of growth. Not only *could* I lead worship, but I loved doing so, and I could see people were responding to this call on my life. Their response to me leading worship, while significant, was secondary to what was most important…this act of worship was a way to come to the throne.

My own devotional life was growing and deepening, but I wasn't yet aware this too was a form of worshipping God. I lived my life in categories—the secular and the sacred. There weren't hard lines or convictions in my journey just yet. This way of approaching my Christianity was popular at the time in the culture I was in, and I never questioned or wondered about it until later in my life.

I eventually met my husband, Jon, in Boston, and we were married. We moved to Martha's Vineyard and became part of a little church where we led worship for three years. The church was such a small congregation that if we weren't there on weekends they'd have no one to do the music. We were very dedicated to this fellowship for those three years and really grew in our faith as well as in our music, but eventually through prayer and a leading of the Lord, we both felt it was time to move to Nashville to pursue Christian music. This is when I really became aware of the meaning of worship.

Charlie Peacock, an artist and producer, had a weekend confer-ence at the Art House that I started attending. One morning as I sat listening to Charlie speak, I began hearing him say things I had never even thought about before. The words he spoke immediately resounded in my heart, and I knew from the response I had that God had been preparing me, aligning me, to hear this word and receive it. The main concept I really grabbed on to during my time at the Art House, was that all of life is lived under the gaze of God, and there is no place God does not exist in our lives…so simple yet so profound. It's funny how just one simple truth can really change the way you live your life.

One of the things the Christian music industry was asking me to do when I moved to Nashville was to define the market I was singing to. In simple terms, they were asking me to describe the people I thought my music would appeal to. I don't know why, but I really had trouble with it and could never arrive at an answer for them. Up until that point in my life, I'd been singing in night clubs, performance halls, and opening for national and regional artists. I never was asked if my music was Christian or non-Christian, I would just do my music. When I'd write I would always stay within the parameters of integrity and didn't worry or think about whether a song communicated a particular message. There was no agenda in my writing on my part; to me it was just art. I felt if I had crafted something well and was passionate about the excellence of the song, I had earned a right to sing before people, whether they agreed with my music or not. Good thing I was always invited back to places. Going out and singing to people in so many different places also gave me amazing opportunities to have conversations about my faith, but again these weren't intentional or forced; it was just something I did, like cooking dinner for friends. I wasn't trying to find an evangelistic platform. The music was a natural part of my life and a natural way to share my faith.

So when I first heard Charlie communicate the whole idea that we are under the gaze of God, it all made sense to me and felt right. I couldn't define my market. I couldn't say I would be drawn to everyone over 60 and would sing only to those women. I had a very dear friend, in the midst of it all, ask me what the difference was between singing on stage and leading people into worship. I found out later he was intentionally asking me a trick question. My response to him was something like, "Well, I think in leading worship I am part of congregational leading, but when I sing my own music I am really opening up a window of who I am inside." His response basically was that there shouldn't be any difference between my leading worship and my singing on stage.

This statement was a real showstopper for me. I actually had to think about what he said, and it wasn't long after he spoke those words to me that I began understanding what he was trying to say. In a nutshell, everything we do needs to point back to God. I may not say the sentence "Oh, this is not about me; this is all about God" when I'm onstage, but I know He's working through me when I'm up there singing, and therefore it's made obvious to those who are watching me sing. If everything truly is under the gaze of God, then everything I do is worship unto Him...everything! Folding laundry, going to work, how I argue with my husband, how I choose to work out my relationships with others—all of this has implications on whether or not I adore God.

This revelation expanded everything in my life. This is now the way I live my life out in Christ. There are places I ought not to go, there are things I should not see or read because I will fall under temptation. I am weak, and I will do things I don't want to do, and say things I don't want to say. Looking at life and God in this new way completely blasted open a new world for me and impacted what I write about and what I communicate in and through my music. I now have new parameters as a result and ask myself when I am writing, does this honor or dishonor Christ? How He uses my music is up to Him. I am free to write anything I want, but as Christ's child, what do I want to write is the real question. I remember reading about Martin Luther and how he had a student come up to him and ask, "Do you mean as a follower of Christ I can do anything I want?" And Martin Luther responded, "Yes, and as a follower of Christ what do you want?" This is really what it is all about, and this question "as a follower of Christ what do you want" has to be at the core of everything we say or do.

So what does worship look like for you today, Diana?

I have two answers, one is more general, and the other more specific. The more general for me is recognizing my day is about God, for God, to God, and through God as Romans 11:36 says, "From him and through him and to him are all things. To him be the glory forever. Amen." I know this in my life, and He proves it to me over and over again. This is now my frame of mind, and my day starts this way whether it is in joy, frustration, or sadness. I do believe Christ has the words of life for us, and as hard as life may get, where else can I go but to Him? This isn't just about me waking up happy every day and worshipping God. It's deciding that whatever my mind-set is, I will choose to worship Him in all things. I feel as though my eyes, my ears, and my mind are tuned in to look for opportunities to talk about Him with my children and with anyone God brings into my path. I really do believe Romans 1:20, "His invisible attributes, namely, his eternal power and divine nature, have been clearly perceived, ever since the creation of the world, in the things that have been made. So they are without excuse."

The more specific application of this change of heart and mind is that I start my day with the people God has put in my life—my husband and my children. I recognize them as from God, and of course my heart is to point them to Him in everything. Let me share about one particular yet pretty typical day around my house. I was exhausted and had only gotten two hours of sleep. I'd been in the studio the night before and then had come home to the work of grading papers for my students. I was functioning on fumes and had little tolerance left. Heading out the door to pick up big sister from school, I noticed little sister had decided to take every stitch of her clothing off. I was irritated and had no patience, and I said to her sternly, "Lina, put your clothes on." But she still just sat there. She wasn't being totally defiant, yet I was in no mood to deal with this ridiculous situation and was so tempted to yell at her. I just wanted to scream, and it was taking everything in me to hold it together to not do so. Finally I just said to her, "Okay, fine, go ahead and come on with no clothes on." Of course she started screaming, "No, Mommy, no!" Frustrated now more than ever, because not only would we be late but we were carpooling and we were making others kids late too, I really came to the end of myself! I didn't have the time to discipline her the way I normally would. I needed her to get up quickly, put on her clothes, and run out the door with me. At that very moment, I heard the Lord say to me, "The anger of man does not produce the righteousness of God."

I immediately thought, *What does that mean? If I can't yell at her right now I don't know what else to do.* So I literally got on my knees and said (by the way, this was no parenting technique; it was simply survival parenting), "Jesus, I don't know what to do because Lina is not obeying, and I am so frustrated." And I started to cry. I'm crying as I am praying. Then Lina looks up at me with her big brown eyes and starts to laugh. She immediately puts her clothes on and we walk to the car. We get in the car and she softly says a prayer. "Lord, help me to obey my mommy." This was so powerful to me, this little bud of faith coming out of my little Lina. Her heart was open to God in such a beautiful way. Did I worship or did I worship? I mean, the whole thing about Him being made perfect in our weakness was communicated right there before my daughter.

I had thankfully refused to give in to my flesh and yell at her or I would have missed this amazing opportunity to actually demonstrate what it means to worship God in all things. It had taken every bit of discipline in me to refrain from yelling at her and forcing her to get in the car. I was so exhausted, I literally didn't know what else to do but fall to my knees in complete submission to God. This is worship. It is complete abandonment to God, allowing Him to be our strength in times of weakness.

Everything we do is about God. Even the most vile images and horrible things people do is somebody's statement about God, whether they intend it to be or not. When you see or hear something awful, we can understand this person does not regard God or the beauty He has created. Everything points to Him.

HOW DO YOU INSERT WORSHIP INTO YOUR PACKED SCHEDULE OF KIDS, LIFE, AND THE BUSYNESS THAT GOES ALONG WITH THEM?

I invite God into every part of my life. I invite Him into my thoughts, my day, and even into this racing mind of mine that never seems to want to stop. I take time in the morning before my day even begins and throughout my day to worship Him. I see worship as intentional moments inserted into my day. For example, I happen to teach preschool, and have the opportunity to lead a devotional every morning, and even though the devotional I read is meant for the kids, I have to say it is pure worship for me...it really is. It is such a joy for me to take the most basic principles of God and make them real to these kids. What a complete joy!

I start my day off with God, and then throughout my day, whenever I am able, I insert worship, prayer, or His Word in or through whatever I am doing. I don't compartmentalize my life and try to make it a ritual. I just make Him a part of everything! I think when we compartmentalize God we risk not seeing Him in all the places He exists. I could be driving along and see a beautiful stream and it could spark worship in me, or I could see a bumper sticker and be reminded of God. Or I could hear a song on the radio that may not necessarily be a song about the Lord, and yet it impacts my faith. These communion moments happen to me in the strangest places. I don't separate the secular and the sacred. I think we really miss out on seeing God and experiencing Him throughout our day when we do that. I don't go to church on Sunday and forget about God the rest of the week. I think about Him and worship Him every day, throughout my day. This is worship to me. This is intimate, life-changing worship and communion with Him, and this is what I will pass on to my children, and to the children at the preschool where I work, and to anyone else I am able to impact in this life.

❋ ❋ ❋

From Diana's great example, we can see how worship encompasses our daily life. It is a pouring out of what has stirred up as a result of our love for God. It is simply an expression of what we feel for Him, and a way to honor Him in all we do.

❧ La Vida Loca ❧

1. Look for ways to worship Him in situations outside of the normal church setting. Go to a park and stand under the trees and sing to Him, or when you are driving down the street sing along with a song that reminds you of the faithfulness of God or His favor and blessing on your life. Turn over a difficult situation to God with prayer and submission right then. Don't limit your worship to just music. See worship as a part of your daily life in all you do.

2. How important is worship in the life of the believer, and why?

3. What are some ways you see worship differently than you did before?

4. Write out your thoughts about God and then say them out loud to Him as a form of worship to Him.

5. Spend time each week worshipping with your children, even if it's singing songs to God in the car.

6. See worship as a form of healing, and when you are worshipping, ask God to heal your heart, your body, your mind.

7. Find ways to spread your sense of worship to your family, friends, children, and neighbors. Have you held back from expressing your faith in certain areas of your life? This is a time to change that!

8. Have you ever experienced pure worship? Have you kept it separate as a "church thing" instead of a "life thing"? Pray about making the transition to a life devoted to worship.

9. Do you divide the secular from the sacred in your life? How can you bring your sense of the sacred to the forefront of all you do or say?

10. What do you want *your* God-crazy style of worship to look like? Feel like?

❧ GOD-CRAZY PRAYER ❧

*L*ord, *help me to* worship You with my heart, with my whole heart. Help me to recognize You in places besides my church, to think of You and worship You all through my day. Lord, open up my eyes to new ways to worship You and honor You, and give me wisdom to teach my children, my family, my friends the same. In Jesus' name. Amen.

16

A New Way to Serve

He made my mouth like a sharpened sword,
in the shadow of his hand he hid me; he made me
into a polished arrow and concealed me in his quiver.
He said to me, "You are my servant Israel, in whom
I will display my splendor."

Isaiah 49:2-3 niv

Over Thanksgiving one year, the kids and I went to Texas to see my family. While visiting the local mall we unexpectedly met a new friend. Mary was sitting quietly on a bench. She didn't express the challenges she was faced with, but we could easily see through the tattered clothes and the expression on her face that Mary needed help. Sure enough, Mary's story was a tragic one. Suffering from a serious bout with diabetes, Mary had to have her foot amputated and was still recovering from the surgery. The bandages were barely covering her leg, and you could see she was not being well taken care of from the discoloration of her skin and the state the bandages were in. Mary had lost her husband of 40 years just weeks before, and someone had broken into her car and stolen most of her belongings, including a special cross necklace he'd given her to remember him by not long before he died.

Mary had not eaten in days and only had a roof over her head because of the generosity of a local police officer who had reached into his own pocket to put her up in a nearby hotel. She had made her way to the mall just to get out and around. My heart immediately went out to her. Standing there with my parents and the kids, I thanked God for this special opportunity He had given to us. This was an opportunity to teach my kids what it means to live out the gospel just as my parents had done in my life. Together we set about getting her some food, and my dad (who has a homeless ministry) got her phone number so he could bring her food through the rest of the week. We wanted to do more; it just didn't seem like enough. Feeling the same way apparently, my mom looked over at me and suggested getting Mary a cross to replace the stolen one her husband had graced her with. There just happened to be a little stand right near us selling crosses, so together we picked one out and my daughter, Madison, eagerly walked over and gave it to her.

How fulfilling it is to be the church as opposed to just doing church or going to church.

Together, the three of us helped her put it on, and as we did, Mary began to cry. My mom, Madison, and I prayed for her right there in the middle of the food court. This moment was church for all of us. I'm sure Mary was thinking about what this meant to her, but all I was thinking about was what it meant to me. These are the types of moments in my life where my heart is transformed, where gratefulness and repentance go hand in hand. God is not condemning me, but His love convicts me to be more Christlike in all I do. His love helps me to know how necessary it is for me to *be* the church in my everyday life. Mary would be fine. At the end of the week she would be on a bus to Tennessee, where her sister had agreed to take care of her, but my daughter, my parents, and I would not be able to just go on with life as usual.

We would be changed forever.

I am trying to learn to be more aware of recognizing these types of souls around me. I get so caught up in the life of my family, my work, my ministry, and just the everyday stuff of life that sometimes I don't see people right in front of me. I am purposely looking for them and waiting for opportunity to serve people like Mary. At this point in my life, I spend my time with people who are focused on living life the same way as I do. I strive to be around men and women who are God focused and who encourage me and keep me accountable to live beyond myself so that I can serve the Lord. Life is too short to spend it any other way. I have much to learn and look forward to it, and I have much to give others and hope to die to my selfish ways in order to do so. This is my journey and oh, how fulfilling it is to be the church as opposed to just doing church or going to church—this is the difference between being an observer in our Christianity, and actually being a God-crazy believer.

Every week, when I walk in to the sanctuary of my church, my desire is that I am ready to *give,* that my cup runneth over. I am not there waiting to *get* something, waiting to receive something from someone. I'm there willing to do whatever is needed to bring value to my fellow believers and to give out of what God has given me.

There are five kids in my family, and we all have the same passion to be the church wherever we may go. Not because we have heard a million sermons, or went to Bible studies or other church functions, or because we are overburdened by our sense of duty or obligation, but because my parents took the time to demonstrate Christianity on a daily basis to five little ones who were always watching. My hope is to hand this mantle down to my children. Teaching them to serve instead of be served, to love beyond what is required, to recognize our finances as merely a tool to help support the work of God, to see worship as an opportunity to connect with Christ in everything we do, and to not live isolated in our walk with God but to find others with the same desire to be authentic and to live life with them.

I grew up being taught the importance of making people feel

welcome and honored. The other day I was trying to teach these principles to my son. I'm always teaching as a mom. The basic word for the day as I drove my kids to school was, "Don't just do what is required when it comes to everything in your life. Go over and above what is required, and you will have great success in all you do." You know what my son said to me? "Mom, I am not going to be a suck-up. Hee, hee, hee." I of course told him this has nothing to do with being a suck-up. This has to be genuine and out of your heart. It's something you do unto God, not for others. Serve out of your faithfulness to Him. Do for others as He asked us to do, and display His splendor along the way.

Serving out of Gratitude

It has taken me many years to figure out *why* I do most things required of the Christian journey. In the beginning of my walk with Christ, I looked around at others to see what a good Christian looked like, dressed like, and even talked like. We have our own Christian lingo, our own acceptable ways that are different in every denomination, and it's sometimes easier to fall into these ways than it is to take time to pursue Him on our own. I believed that by mimicking others who were more spiritually mature, I would draw closer to God. When that didn't necessarily work, I began to do things to draw me closer to God. I went to Bible studies, became active in my church, went to women's events, Wednesday night service, and did all the things I felt God wants from the good Christian. I wanted to please God, and this was the only way I knew how. This doing, doing, doing is what I saw around me, so this must be the way to the heart of God.

It was not only my desire to emulate other Christians and please God, I also wanted to win the whole world for Jesus and save the lost. Because I was saved out of the pit of sin, I would rerun my life's mental video time and time again, reminding myself of who I was before I knew Christ. I felt indebted to Christ forever. I wanted to repay God for all He had done for me. I committed early on that I would give my life to Him and to His purposes, whatever that meant all the days of my life. So I did things I thought would please God.

My motives were pure, but the actions born out of them were a bit misguided. I can recognize now how these were all outward things. They were good for me and helped me grow, but they did not create intimacy with the Father. God doesn't need us to do anything for Him, He desires us to not "do" but "be." "Be still, and know that I am God" (Psalm 46:10). Know Him, love Him, worship Him, serve Him, and fellowship with those who do. This is all that is required.

I had never experienced a close relationship with my own father until much later in life, and it was hard for me to envision myself being completely intimate and close with my heavenly Father. The big question is why? Why me? Why would God, the Creator of the ends of the earth want a relationship with me? Why?

I remember sitting with Bruce Wilkinson (who wrote the best-selling book *Prayer of Jabez*) in a little restaurant in Fort Worth, Texas, and saying to him, "Bruce, I do not feel I can really get close to God. I want to, but I feel so unworthy to really go into the throne room, to really walk hand in hand with the Almighty God."

Quietly and with great confidence, Bruce told me that I was not worthy, and I was not ever going to be worthy; it is only in Christ we are made worthy. It is through Him and the power of the Holy Spirit that we are able to draw close to God. I have been made worthy, and I can commune with Him in the Holy of Holies.

Wow! What a response. I was encouraged during and immediately after that conversation. But then as I settled back in to my ordinary life, my pattern of doing and going, I didn't believe it. In the depths of my heart, in the stillness of those moments when I sought God's heart, I did not believe God truly cared whether He had a close relationship with me.

When will we learn that we cannot ever earn God's love? When will we understand that serving has nothing to do with what we will give, but has everything to do with what we will receive. When we become a believer in Christ and embrace the God-crazy life, our hearts are transformed, and our love for Christ will drive our passion to serve, to give to others, and to make a difference on this earth. So the question you may ask is, "Do I have to serve?" and the question I would ask you in return is, "Can you love Christ and not serve?" For if we love our Lord, then we will want to serve Him and others around us.

God-Crazy Service: Donna's Story

I met Donna one afternoon visiting Mercy Children's Clinic. I had been asked to join the board of directors and was being given a tour of the facility. The heart of the ministry of Mercy immediately resonated with me. It's a clinic established to serve the needs of the poor by pulling from the resources of the blessed. That in itself was not as impressive as the way they run the clinic with such quality care, and go above and beyond to make families feel loved and cared for. Not only do they meet their physical needs by providing top quality physician care, but they pray for the needs of these families and even help with other resources they might need.

When I was introduced to Donna, I could see immediately that she had a deep joy in her and about her. I was curious about her inner joy and the way she seemed to express it in her actions and her presence. In her role as a nurse at the clinic, she was fulfilling her opportunities to serve, but I felt her passion to serve went above and beyond her paycheck, and I soon found out I was right. Here is Donna's story in her own words.

I grew up as the youngest of six kids; we had different fathers. I was born when my mother was 45 years old and suffered complete abandonment and abuse throughout my childhood...going from home to home. I was told I would never amount to anything. Through it all God surrounded my life and protected me. I never received love, and that is why I personally know the power of prayer, and why I am so determined to pray for others. It is the way I serve.

I accepted Christ at 11 years old. If I had not made that commitment, I don't know where I would be now. I know God has everything to do with me being here today. When I became a teenager, I began memorizing chapters of the Bible, and I sought the Lord with all my heart. I love the Word of God, and I know it is powerful and real. It transforms people's lives; it transformed mine. I am still working through healing from my past. All my family is deceased except for a sister and an estranged brother. No one survived the circumstances of our upbringing the way I have, and I know it has been the Lord who has sustained me.

If my horrible upbringing wasn't enough to kill me, I went to live with my pastor, and he took advantage of me sexually. I was so desperate for a father I didn't say anything and wanted him to be my father. The longing in my heart was so great, I did not care about what he was doing. Finally, I grew to understand that this relationship was wrong. I confronted people around me and ended up moving. It was a very depressing time for me, but again God saw me through.

The one thing I had going for me was my mind. I was blessed with intelligence. It's the one thing that delivered me from my hell. Teachers saw this gift in me and helped me get a full-ride scholarship to college. It's definitely what saved me. While this opportunity was a blessing, after college, with a low self-esteem, I married a man who was abusive and on drugs. A few years later I was divorced with two kids. This is when my past finally caught up with me. I realized I had been sexually abused my whole life, and everything began to take its toll on me. The abuse, the divorce, the abandonment, all came to a head, and the only thing that saved me once again was my passion to be close to God. I consumed myself with the things of God and asked Him to give me wisdom and be my lifeline.

Out of the pain I found myself crying and rejoicing at the same time. This is the way it is in our Christian journey. We may find ourselves in trials, and yet if we reach out to Him, we will find ourselves rejoicing in the trial. This is where the joy comes from. It is not in me to rejoice, but it is not I, but it is Christ who lives in me, who delivers me from my trials.

Today, my passion to serve comes from this deep joy that no one could place there but God. I so desire to help other women, who may be experiencing the some of the same things I did as a young girl and as a young woman. My journey has not been easy. My ministry is prayer, and I pray and intercede for many who are wounded or who are downcast. I love serving, and I don't take for granted one moment of my life. He has provided for me, protected me, and healed me, and now just like the many people He set free in His Word, I will go out and serve Him and tell others the good news of how He is able to deliver us from evil.

❈ ❈ ❈

Donna radiates the love of God. You would never know she has endured the trials we only touched on in this interview. It was difficult for me to sit through the interview with a dry eye, hearing about the pain she had endured as a young girl. She finally reached over and placed her hand on mine, comforting me, and letting me know it is no longer a source of pain for her. Amazing. She was comforting me, when it would seem as though she needed the comfort. Out of Donna's heart to serve comes the transformation of many people's lives—including mine. She touched my heart, and I saw her deep passion for prayer in the brief moments we spent together.

She is not serving God out of obligation or out of duty, but rather out of her tremendous love for Him and out of her unwavering belief in how much He loves her, cares for her, protects her, and has fought for her life. Yes, fought for her. God has fought for us all, battling the enemy and taking back the ground on the cross so Jesus could be a substitute and sacrifice to atone our sins. This inspires in us a passion to serve Him and to radiate His splendor when we do.

❧ La Vida Loca ❧

1. Have you found a passion for serving? What has serving meant to you in the past?

2. What inspires you and opens up your heart in a way that seems beyond human capacity? Is it when you help children? When you teach? When you give financially? When you see someone's unique gifts and you encourage them?

3. List or think through times when someone else's fulfillment of passion for service has touched your life, changed your life, or impacted your own journey of purpose.

4. Are you using your gifts and talents in a way that displays His splendor?

5. When have you felt unworthy of God's love or healing? When have you felt unworthy of having a unique and wonderful purpose?

6. List some of the ways you have seen God show His love to you, His pursuit of you? How does acknowledging these things make you feel?

7. Serving doesn't look the same to everyone. How does serving look to you?

8. When has God fought for you?

9. Look at your calendar. How much of what you do is done out of obligation?

10. The God-crazy life is about discovery. Are you living your life as though you still have more to know, discover, embrace, and learn about you and God? If not, what needs to change?

❧ GOD-CRAZY PRAYER ❧

Lord, give me a deep understanding of Your care for my life and my hurts and my past and my present and my future. Fill me with the truth of Your love so that I do not seek to fill that from any other source. May my desire to serve be born of my heart for You and for Your sacrifice. May it rise up and direct me as my purpose becomes even more clear. Keep me from false priorities or false pride that sway me toward saying yes to the wrong things. Reveal to me those who serve out of a passionate love for You so that I will have models of what it means to live abundantly and with God-crazy devotion. In Jesus' name. Amen.

17

A New Way to Connect with Others

Sisters in Christ are as precious as flowers. Each one is different in her own unique way. Each one blooms in her own unique time. And they come together to make a beautiful, sweet-smelling bouquet.

—Michelle Borquez

Women today need to connect on a real level with other women who will help them walk through the daily tasks, struggles, and challenges of their lives. We need one another! Relationships are vital in the life of each and every God-crazy woman. Our inter-dependence on one another is also an expression of our complete dependence on God. I believe that women understand a bit more than men do how much we need the people God places in our lives. Sometimes we need people to serve. Sometimes we need to humbly accept the service of another. There are moments when our hunger for church is filled by the generous spirit of a friend or the comforting squeeze of the hand by a stranger moved by empathy.

So if we need one another for our own spiritual growth and survival, then why do we have the tendency to feel we are in competition with one another? Every one of us is unique, and yet we compare ourselves to one another as if we were all meant to be the same. It's what I call comparison shopping. While this might be considered discerning when buying a car or a new dress, it is destructive when we are trying on identities that are not our own or striving to become something we are not.

When we compare ourselves to each other, we are taking away from our chance to celebrate our own uniqueness in Christ.

Do you ever walk into a room and the first thing you do is compare yourself with everyone there? Or have you heard someone share about their experience and then immediately felt pressure to be just like them? It's easy to do this when we are new wives or new parents. Everyone either has advice or stories to share. We take a lot of mental notes during these life transitions because we want to be good, acceptable, and approved. There is nothing wrong with learning from others, which we'll talk about shortly, but these comparisons are rarely about gleaning godly wisdom. They are often born out our insecurities and nurtured by our fears of falling short of someone's expectations.

God-crazy women know the secret to authentic, meaningful, and pure relationships. They pursue God's expectations and His alone. This is absolute freedom, my friend. When your life is only about resting in God's strength and pleasing Him, you can enter into a conversation without motives that alter the very course of that conversation. Encounters with strangers or friends can be all about sharing the gifts of hospitality, good listening, and acceptance. We can be ourselves—uniquely put together and gifted and blessed by God to carve out our special path in this lifetime and to serve the kingdom.

We've discussed before how we can be lenient, forgiving, and grace-giving to friends but so filled with criticism for ourselves. When will we learn? Those of us who are mothers have little excuse to dismiss the concept of individuality, unique personalities, and gifting. We see it clearly in the demeanors, talents, and charms of our own children. From the time my first son, Josh, was born, I knew he was a strong kid. He never slept and still doesn't. I would try to get him to take a nap, but it was useless. I would call friends, and they would tell me how their little one was down for a nap and how great it was to take a break. I couldn't understand why my little guy wouldn't even close his eyes for a moment. He would wake up every morning crying because he immediately wanted out of bed. Even though Josh didn't need a lot of sleep, he did need a lot of food. He loved eating as a baby, and he loves eating as a teenager now. However, Aaron, my secondborn, slept through the night within the first few weeks of birth (Josh was up every night for a year and a half). Aaron slept so much my neighbors would tease me, telling me they knew I didn't really have another baby. When he woke up in the morning, I'd have to go in and check to see if he was awake. He wouldn't make a peep. His big brown eyes were wide open and he would just lie there patiently waiting for me to come get him. He ate so little I was concerned he wasn't eating enough; he still is not a big eater today. Josh and Aaron both have different needs and different wants, and I consider these when making decisions about them. If I treated them both the same or even held the same expectations for both, I would not be acknowledging what I know to be true about them—they are different and wonderful and unique. They are my boys...but they are each God's child with his own purpose.

I remember being pregnant with Madison, my daughter, not knowing, of course, she would be a girl, thinking to myself and wondering how this next baby would be different from the other two. I thought the same thing when my youngest son, Jacob, came along. Not only would these last two be different, they were practically opposites. I used to look in the rearview mirror of my then minivan (I have been delivered, ladies) many times to see Josh and Aaron grunting and griping over the exuberance and laughter of my younger two. They'd say things like, "Mom, tell them to be quiet. Why do they have to be sooo loud?" Of course, Madison and Jacob were born laughing, singing, and not too much later… dancing. What has been amazing as they have grown older is to see their gifts impact my life in ways so innate to their personalities. Josh is my rock, my foundation. Aaron makes me laugh and loves to challenge my thinking along with his older brother. I have always called Madison and Jacob my joy babies. They bring me so much joy with their little outrageous personalities. Each one of my children, while so different, is a piece to a much greater puzzle—our family. I cannot even imagine one of them out of our family puzzle. It would create a huge hole and an imbalance to our life.

When we compare ourselves to each other, we are taking away from our chance to celebrate our own uniqueness in Christ. We all have different needs, different gifting, and different purposes here on this earth. This is important to realize when stepping out to create meaningful or lasting relationships. We are not alike, and we shouldn't begin to pursue a relationship with the desire to either become just like that person or to turn that person into us. It just won't work! I let my kids know, "It takes one hundred percent of your time to take care of you, so don't worry about what everyone else is doing!" Same goes for us. Focus on *you* changing and not changing others, and *you* will do just fine. God created us all as unique children because we are an important single piece of the greater puzzle…the body of Christ. Without you, the greater picture would not be complete, nor would it be as lovely.

God-Crazy Relationships: Alicia's Story

Alicia is in her late twenties with two children. She recently expressed to me her desire to see change in the way we, as a church and as *the* church, live when it comes to depending on one another and doing relationships. This is her viewpoint in her own words.

I really love God. I think I always have in my fatally flawed, seriously fallen way. I love His Word, though at times I find it to be incredibly difficult to understand. I love His creation; I find it beautiful and humorous and totally, well, creative. And because He is so good and I am so not good, it seems unbelievable that He could tolerate me, let alone love me. But the Bible says He does, and I believe it. Praise God!

I come from a long line of God-lovers. These are not just church-goers, but true lovers of Christ. My mother and father pray for their children earnestly. It is from them that I feel I learned the most about God. Church, on the other hand, was more like a safe place where I could meet other people who looked and behaved very much like me. What I remember most is the cleanliness of the building and the niceness of the people. And that's great! I really loved that and I am grateful to my church and to my parents for bringing us there. I do think, however, that this comfort can be lulling and addictive. I believe it can keep us from the only thing that is worth anything in this life—knowing Jesus Christ.

God is not nice and safe. When I finally started reading the Bible out of a true desire to know God, He was faithful to begin to reveal Himself. He is not bound by anything. The wildness of God's nature, the recklessness of Christ's sacrifice, and the power of the Spirit's comfort began to move me so deeply I was changed. And that is huge! As humans, we do not change automatically. We have to be moved to change, and God does move us, but He does it on His terms and in His way. The amazing thing about this is how alive we feel when we remove our clammy little fists from the steering wheel of our life. This kind of letting go doesn't tend to happen when we feel nice and safe.

I dream of church being different. I dream of it being a safe place for people who don't look and behave like me—but how to get there, I have no idea. I have questions I ask, though. When did we start separating ourselves into age groups and common circumstances for Sunday school and Bible study? Do we think that segregation is a good way to do life? Why is church such a busy, stressful place that leaves families feeling exhausted? How did our churches get so huge? When did we start pretending we have to be good all the time? Why are people outside the church so terrified of going in? There must be a real reason. And when did we get so terrified of them? They are just lost and in need of a Shepherd. They're not scary. Why does every family member have to go someplace different to feel connected? What makes it so hard for us as Christians to invest in each other's lives without forced fellowship groups?

I desire connection that isn't fabricated. I desire the kind of unity that flows from the reality of the gospel. We are subjects in a kingdom where our King is also the one who came into our hell and fought madly to bring us back. This should arrest us. We are dead to wonder. We are dead to this magnificent and intimate truth. We need Christ desperately. We need Him desperately. Only He can open our eyes, clean out our ears, soften our hearts, and give us fresh desire to want Him. When we truly want Christ, when nothing but His presence will do, when we are desperate for Him, then nice and safe will no longer do.

❊ ❊ ❊

The Relationships We Need

Some of our relationships will be with women in the church and some will be with those who are seekers or coworkers or neighbors or fellow room-parents at our kids' schools. They can begin with one comment, moment of solidarity, or even a moment of conflict. It's healthy to have a variety of friendships, but when you desire to foster relationships with other God-crazy women, here are some vital traits to watch for in the other person:

1. She does not have a personal agenda and isn't self-absorbed or driven for self-gain.

2. She allows you to fail and talks about her own failures and weaknesses.

3. She realizes the importance of doing life with others and isn't just a fair-weather friend.

4. She mentors, she is mentored, and she cares for others' needs (serving and loving with compassion).

5. She is an encourager and is not negative and does not put down others around her.

6. She has nothing bad to say of others and doesn't gossip (and quickly repents if she does).

7. She looks for opportunities to give.

8. She draws from the "tree of life," not the world for her affirmation.

9. She will sacrifice her own needs and wants when it is appropriate to do so.

10. She believes family is second to God. She sees her responsibility as mother and wife as more than that of caring for physical needs, but also to the spiritual needs they have. She makes a home.

11. She considers money, fame, and/or leadership to be opportunities for her to influence others for God—not opportunities for self-gain.

12. She sees her desperate need for God and engages in His embrace.

13. She welcomes people into her home and does not place material things over the importance of people.

14. She is not stuck in the muck of her past, but she has forgiven and looks to the future or is at least in the process of doing so.

15. She is intentional in living out God's Word by not being one who only observes, but also one who engages in making a difference and displaying God's splendor.

16. She has a strong sense of purpose. She isn't hanging out waiting for others to serve her. She is not selfish.

17. She has abandoned self-agenda and has a God-agenda. She does things out of the abundance of her heart and not out of a sense of obligation.

18. She is mature enough to admit when she is wrong, and will work through the obstacles in your relationship in order for the relationship to go deeper.

19. She is loyal to those she loves, so if you end up going to the mud, she will be right there with you.

20. She is a woman of faith and prayer!

These are the things to be looking for when you form one of the three essential kinds of relationships in a God-crazy woman's life—a mentoring relationship in which you are mentored, an equal partnership, or a mentoring relationship in which you mentor another woman or girl. These specific relationships will help you get through your life with fulfillment, design, intent, and hope for all that God has created for you.

The Mentor

Howard Schultz, CEO of Starbucks, has often shared the core principles for the company's success: Don't be threatened by people smarter than you. Compromise anything but your core values. Seek to renew yourself, even when you are hitting home runs. Everything matters.

When we are not threatened by people who are smarter, we can learn and grow. The first relationship we all need is a mentor and what I call a "safe" relationship. This is not an easy relationship to find. I have been blessed to have at least one mentor during most times in my adult life. Here is what to look for in a mentoring situation:

1. Look for a woman who is humble and has been through trials. She will not easily judge you in your situation, but instead she will offer sound advice.

2. Don't find a mentor in your immediate family. They cannot help but be biased. It's fine to take advice and talk freely with your mother, but don't unload everything in your life on her, and don't expect her to always give you advice that will challenge you. She will naturally want to protect and baby you.

3. Make sure whomever you choose is safe. By that I mean someone you can completely trust. You may want to use a woman counselor who is a Christian for this relationship. You need to be able to expose your sin and turn from it. Exposing your sin is very important in the God-crazy life. Hidden sin can eventually destroy us and those around us.

4. Look for a woman who is not competitive and who does not envy others.

5. Seek a mentor who will not make you feel less valued for being different.

6. It is very important your mentor understands the concept of allowing others to live out process in order to grow. You need to be able to fail without condemnation and with sound advice, compassion, and mercy. Trading the treasure of hope for the fear of condemnation will not offer you restoration.

7. Find someone who really loves you and gets you.

Why a mentor? We do not need to be left to our own counsel, and in order to grow in godliness and righteousness, we need someone who has gone before us leading us down the path they have once walked. Has a friend ever called you on your bad behavior? Or have they ever sat down with you and thoughtfully, prayerfully discussed your faith walk? This won't be just any friend or just any woman in your life who can do such things. We need those mentors!

A wise woman certainly understands the importance of good

counsel. When you receive life-giving and soul-stretching insight, it will protect you from many of life's trappings and from destructive behaviors. It will also bring blessing to you and your family as you seek to improve in areas of weakness. Find a mentor who is strong in areas you are not, and don't be afraid to expose your weaknesses to her. You need someone who is going to shoot straight with you and not just tell you what you want to hear.

A Sista Who Is an Equal

This girl had better be fun. Why an equal? Well, I have found it is important to have someone who is in the same place in life as you are to really get ya. My dear friend Tammy is a good example. We both have four kids. We've been through the trials of marriage. And we love fashion, good food, and the ultimate requirement—lots of laughter. When the two of us get together and others come along, we are one big party to go. Our joy in being together and in being God crazy is contagious. We love to laugh and cut up!

Another benefit of having this kind of friend is that your life language is very similar. There are times when I need only look at Tammy to know what is going on in her mind, heart, and life at that moment. We can express ourselves openly, and the other knows just how to respond and empathize. When a friendship is strengthened by common threads, you will experience true camaraderie and will be able to speak into each others lives and be a support for one another.

Mentoring Another

I have mentored many young women, and I can tell you that this practice, discipline, and delight of mentoring has brought me great joy. I have been able to see these girls or young women grow up, get married, and implement things I handed down to them. They did not see a perfect being in me, but they did see a woman wanting to be made perfect in the image of God. Reread that line. It's an important distinction. In fact, we should also always be reminding ourselves of this truth. It will help us release our actual failures to the Lord and let go of those perceived failures which emerge when we try to be perfect on our own.

There is such a need for older women to mentor the younger ones. Look for girls and young women to take under your wing and mentor. Young ladies whose mothers are not around will especially need this support, but I can tell you that every girl and every woman benefits from someone other than their relatives taking an interest in them, their growth as a woman, and their spiritual journey. It is worth the sacrifice. You will receive more than you give.

I know that offering to be a mentor can be as intimidating as asking to be mentored. We are afraid we will let someone else down or even worse—be responsible for their downfall! Such pressure we put on ourselves to be every thing to every one we have a relationship with. You might be good at talking with and listening to a girl who rarely gets the captive attention of an adult. That is a gift and a great start in the mentoring process. Maybe you have special talents, such as cooking, crafts, writing, athletics, or business skills that you can pass along to a woman with the desire to learn. You see, you don't have to do it all, but you do have to make yourself available for this process to begin. It will change her life and your life, and I believe it will then, in turn, change many other lives because you will both take away a deep understanding of how vital it is to support one another in prayer, conversation, commitment, and relationship.

It is so important we do life together as believers. It is easy to isolate ourselves and stay inside our own worlds, but it is only in the getting out and giving of ourselves that we can truly receive all God meant for us when it comes to relationships. We need one another. We cannot always overcome on our own. I know what it is like to isolate yourself and let people see only what you want them to see... remember I did that. It is not the way God created us to live. He created us for relationships, and while there is risk, there is much more to gain when we come together as the body of Christ.

❧ LA VIDA LOCA ❧

1. What type of friendships do you have now? What are you missing?

2. What attributes of a God-crazy woman do you need to work on?

3. Why have relationships failed in the past?

4. What means the most to you in a friendship and why?

5. What are some ways to form friendships that have worked for you?

6. Who has been a mentor in your life? If you did not have a mentor, was a woman role model present in your life at an important time?

7. Which one of your deep dark fears keeps you from connecting to other women? Do you realize that they are probably grappling with the very same fear?

8. Pray for your sista-in-partnership friend. If you don't have someone who shares some of your life circumstances and values, pray that God will lead you to that woman.

9. Be watching for whom you can mentor. Maybe it is someone you have not yet met. Yet again, it might be a young woman who has been in your life all along. As risky as it seems, take the leap of faith and develop a relationship with that young girl.

10. What can you learn from God's faithfulness in your own life that can help you embrace and nourish your relationships?

❧ GOD-CRAZY PRAYER ❧

Lord, I can feel so alone, even when I'm surrounded by my family and my church family. Help me reach beyond my insecurities so that You can show me, once again, how faithful You are when Your children take a step forward in their faith. Protect me from bad relationships, reveal to me those relationships which need mending, and point me toward those friendships that are ready to bloom. In Jesus' name. Amen.

18

GOD CRAZY AT LAST

I stand at the edge of the ocean and hear Your voice in the sea.
I shout in the midst of a canyon, and You call back to me.
I sit at the top of a mountain, and see Your face in the land.
So why do I doubt and wonder, if my life is in Your hands?

—MICHELLE

My life has been a process of learning to trust in Him for all things. From the first step of submission to God crazy, this process has been an awakening to the sweet aroma and joy of the wholly surrendered life. God delights in the surrendered woman's pure heart, speech, actions, purpose, and pursuit. She is less interested in religion and more interested in her heart reflecting the love of Christ. She expresses His purposes and His love to those around her. Her failures and disappointments have not held her back, but instead they have moved her forward because she knows God has redeemed what was meant to destroy her. The God-crazy woman dances and shouts with joy because she has surrendered. She is free!

> When one turns to the Lord, the veil is removed. Now the
> Lord is the Spirit, and where the Spirit of the Lord is, there
> is freedom. And we all, with unveiled face, beholding

glory of the Lord, are being transformed into the same image from one degree of glory to another. For this comes from the Lord who is the Spirit (2 Corinthians 3:16-18).

Not a Separate Life

Do you ever feel as though your life has a secular side and a sacred one? Our transformed life is a whole life. The sacredness of God is displayed in and through all we do as we give honor to Him and praise to His name. When we walk in our calling and use our gifting to glorify Him, those lines that used to separate behaviors or thoughts or viewpoints into the secular and the sacred categories do not exist because there is no secular side to a God-crazy woman. Those around you will be surprised how you can be so confident and purposed in the world, but be all about God and His calling on your life. Christians and non-Christians alike will want to know the secret to such complete, abundant living. His gaze is upon us always.

God longs for you to take the ride of your life.

If you are a God-crazy person…everything happens out of a heart that is surrendered. There is no existence apart from Christ. Whether you are in full-time ministry or you are a businesswoman, a musician, a mom, a teacher, or any combination of these, your life and your life's work will flow with and demonstrate the love of Christ. We will have times when we absolutely hunger for time alone with Christ so we can seek Him and fill ourselves up with His love. But in the other times, when we are going about our days or thinking on big life decisions or the most mundane list of errands, we are also in God's presence. We are spending time with God every step of our day when our heart is tethered to His in God-crazy fashion. What is so especially wonderful about this point in your adventure is that you will suddenly realize that your mind quickly leaps to thoughts of God and prayer. Before God-crazy surrender, we often have to be reminded to think on Him and His Word or to lift up our prayers. Life becomes an ongoing time of communion with the Lord.

It is a great loss when the Christian journey becomes a religious obligation or something we do on autopilot because it is an engrained habit or an expectation of others. In the old life when you were planning every step, worrying about tomorrow's destination, and trying to wrangle the control of the car from God's safe hands, this sense of religious routine was more likely to take hold. Your new, living faith is more organic as a natural expression of the new heart you have for God and His heart. Everything is for Him, through Him, and with Him but without the obligation and guilt that accompanies a legalistic faith that forgets the power of the resurrection and has embraced only rules and regulations.

Your pursuit of a love relationship with the Lord will translate into a desire to help others, give to others, and lay down your agenda so people can see Him in you. We are all gifted in different ways, and our significance and power to be effective comes from the One who lives within us, not from what we do for a living or how the world might label us. Pour yourself into your gifts and allow Him to be seen as you express yourself in what you do. It is all "ministry." It is all honorable.

Do you feel God's pursuit of you and see the evidence of it as you look over your life? Think back to that field where we started our journey and the beautiful display of all God wants to bestow upon you. God longs for you to take the ride of your life, allowing Him to direct you in the ways you should go. He is there loving you, proud of who you are, and the woman He has created you to become.

I am finally in a good place. Not a perfect place, not a place where there is no more to learn (because there is always more to learn), but it is a place where I stand firmly in the knowledge of who my God is. I will dance with Him in His arms, and all things around me will become faint, as if I were dancing with my lover.

He is the lover of my soul and wants the best for me. When I insist on detours, He takes me back time and time again.

Has God taken you back over and over again? Do you feel there are no more chances? He is always there with loving and open arms. It is never too late to fall for God. We have fallen for so many things, things that do not satisfy, and now let's fall for Him completely. The Creator of the universe, who formed and knit us together in our mother's womb, knows every hair on our head and the very secrets we hold in our uniqueness because He planted them there. Can you even imagine it? Not ever being turned away from His loving arms. No rejection, no embarrassment. Just true grace, mercy, and a deep love for you.

Entrusting the Rest of Your Journey

As a parent I knew from the very beginning that I wanted trust to be the foundation for my relationship with my children. Maintaining that trust is an ongoing process. The kids have to see it and feel it to believe it. And it is the same for the parents. We watch our kids and their behavior to observe how they are thriving in the trust we have given to them. In my family I let my kids know that even if I don't agree with them on an issue, I am still open to letting them be heard, and I even allow them the opportunity to possibly change my mind on an issue. This openness has created an environment of safety for them to share their feelings and ideas without being shut down. I had been afraid that when they entered their teen years they would probably cut me off, but I have been so blessed that they have entrusted their fears as well as their dreams to me. It is a great responsibility and privilege to be trusted so deeply.

In our relationship with God, if we thought His love was contingent upon us being perfect rather than us being perfected in Him through the Holy Spirit, we wouldn't feel freedom to come to Him when in trouble or in pain as a result of our sin or misjudgments. Other than having to know Christ personally, we do not have to be prequalified to be used by God or to live the God-crazy life. And each time we fail, we do not need a mediator or a lawyer to state our case before His throne because we are already free in His grace. We do not have to be sinless or get our life together. We just have to trust Him enough to surrender to Him, and in our surrender we find Him and fall in love with Him. We can come to Him in our darkest hour, and we can dream with Him in the greatest moments of our lives.

In the Bible story of the prodigal son, the father could see the son walking toward him from far away. Instead of making the wayward child walk to him, the father ran to the son and they walked the remaining distance together. Jesus accompanies us even when we have lost our way and are stranded along a dark side road that was never meant to be a part of our journey. He gets us back to the safety of His plan and His direction, all the while teaching us wisdom and with His example of unconditional love.

Carried to Surrender

A dear friend came to visit recently. We had not seen each other in more than a year and had a lot to catch up on. While sitting at a local Starbucks, she began to open up about the amazing things God had been doing in her life. Right in front of me was an incredible example of a clearly surrendered woman. She had battled alcoholism for years and her burden had been heavy; this demon almost destroyed her life. But then the Lord had given her a sweet vision of His great love. It was the image of my friend carrying her three-year-old daughter in her arms. Her daughter's face was buried on her shoulder and her arms were wrapped tightly around her mama's body as if holding on for dear life. My friend was walking with her and carrying her as if to keep her safe from harm. She knew God was carrying her with this love.

What a beautiful picture for all of us to think on. This is exactly what engaging in God's loving embrace would look and feel like. Our arms wrapped tightly around Him as we depend on Him for our existence, purpose, and every need. We turn toward Him and bury our face in His shoulder, comforted and protected. This is not only the picture of pure love, it is the image of surrender God's way. Unlike the world's idea of surrender, which evokes images of force or the breaking of another's spirit, God's call to surrender is His offer to carry us, shelter us, and lead us, with His arms around us all the while. Close your eyes and imagine this form of surrender. This is the way to God crazy...it is peaceful, inviting, and radically different from the world's offering. It is joyful and beautiful, and it draws us closer to the heart of our Creator where the adventure truly begins.

Lord, help us joyfully surrender our hearts. Give us a longing for You, hungry for all You have to give us. Amen.

Our Epitaph

I had a sobering experience walking through one of the oldest settlements in the South, Cades Cove, located in the Great Smoky Mountains. In this vast wilderness more than 200 years ago people fought against the elements, unknown diseases, and wild animals. The photos from that era show how this untamed land took its toll. As I walked through the cabins and the churches dating back to the early 1800s, I had such a range of emotion as I thought about all the women of that era and what they had to endure. But it wasn't until I went to the graveyard that it really hit me.

All that's known about Mary Sparks is that she was born in 1869 and she departed in 1936. The epitaph on her faded small gravestone read like this: "Was blind here. Now I see the beauty of heaven." Such a simple statement. As I stood there, staring, imagining, feeling, and sensing the brevity of life like few times before, here was all I knew about Mary: She lived at least her last days in darkness. By the epitaph you can tell that Mary had a dream and a hope that after this life she would behold the beauty of heaven!

Jesus made one of His most controversial statements in the Sermon on the Mount in Matthew 6:23-34. He said, "If the light that is in you is darkness, how great is this darkness. No one can serve two masters." He is saying that it's one thing to be deceived, but it's a whole other level of deception to believe you are walking in the light and in reality you are in the dark. So, just who is this person? It's the person who is serving two masters. It's the person who is straddling both light and darkness and trying to make it work. The God-crazy life is not a divided life. It's complete, united, and focused on the one and only Master of life and light.

Mary, according to the epitaph, is now beholding the beauty of heaven and that is wonderful. But, Jesus said we could experience the reality of heaven right here on the earth. While Mary gazed on heaven once she left this earth, we are told we can gaze on heaven while we are still here. So how do we catch a glimpse of heaven? By allowing the God-crazy life to unfold in our lives and by yielding ourself to the tight embrace our Father so longs to give us.

This life, this God-crazy life, is simply put…the Jesus years. Girls, we never arrive. We keep on being a passenger along for the ride of a lifetime, and while we are tempted to get in the driver's seat each time we face a traffic jam, we finally begin to surrender to the fact that we will never be as good a driver as the one who loves us best, Jesus Himself. Our joy comes from the assurance that we can sit back and savor the ride—no more trying to control it, no more trying to figure it all out. We can have peace knowing He's got it all under control and the road trip is going to be so much better than we ever thought possible. Better snacks, better vacations—even the detours are remarkable with Him at the wheel of our lives.

Hang on and get ready for a great adventure. As sisters in Christ, we are in this together. The God-crazy life plan rests in His hands and will be a journey you and I can embrace and celebrate.

❧ LA VIDA LOCA ❧

1. Do you trust God? If not, what holds you back? If so, how will you let that trust change your life?

2. Did your living faith turn to religion at some point? Have you moved out of that place of rules and regulations and returned to abundant, God-crazy belief?

3. How do you see yourself and your purpose differently after going through this book?

4. Think of a time when you felt energized by your longing for Christ. Using the tools in this book and the experiences of our journey together, how will you keep that pursuit of Christ alive?

5. Is your heart open? Is there mortar around it, keeping others out and you from really living out God's purpose in your life?

6. What places in your life still need healing? What people or problems or attitudes keep you on the side of the road?

7. Think on the beautiful image of surrender my friend shared with me. Imagine yourself being carried by God all the days of your life. Relax into this thought, this truth, and this great, deep love. This is God-crazy surrender that awaits you.

8. How has your view of worship, service, and connection changed by observing the heart and mind-set of the God-crazy women in these chapters?

9. What excites you about being on this journey now?

10. What are some of your biggest hopes for your God-crazy adventure? List them, pray for them, and ultimately give them over to God with a surrendered heart. Let Him mold them into the adventure He has planned for you. Remember...nothing will compare!

❧ GOD-CRAZY PRAYER ❧

Lord, it has been long since I have sat at Your feet. I am so thankful for You. Every step I take, every breath I have is for You to use. You are faithful to me even when I am not faithful to You. Like a heavy rain pouring down from heaven above, Your love comes down upon me. I lift my eyes to You as you hold me in Your arms, carrying me through the dark places in life. Lord, help my hands to be kind for You. Help me see people through Your eyes so I can reach out to them in love. Lord, grant me favor even with my enemies and help my heart to remain pure and my words honest. Give me strength to resist storing up treasures of this world so I can embrace the treasures of Your kingdom. Help my hunger and thirst to be quenched only by You. Let Your love be displayed in my being. Rebuild the broken places of my life and heal me in my woundedness. Keep my heart open before You and please chip away at any mortar that remains within it. Break through with Your love. Place in my life a passion like I have never had before and the power to press into the things You have for me. Who would have need for anything more once they have felt Your amazing embrace? Thank You for being my Friend and my Savior, and help me to surrender all to You so I can remain Your humble servant. In Your precious name. Amen.

Other Great Books for God-Crazy Women

WHAT HAPPENS WHEN WOMEN SAY YES TO GOD
by Lysa TerKeurst

Lysa TerKeurst shares inspiring stories from her own life along with compelling biblical insights as she describes the deep joy and great purpose of a life that honors God.

EXPERIENCE THE ULTIMATE MAKEOVER
by Sharon Jaynes

Readers will discover that true beauty is really all about what goes on inside a woman. In letting God transform their hearts, minds, wills, and emotions, readers will see that knowing the supreme Makeover Artist will help them become everything they are meant to be.

SASSY GIRL'S GUIDE TO LOVING GOD
by Michelle McKinney Hammond

What makes the difference between merely existing in this life and living each day with excitement and passion? Our love relationship with God! Michelle McKinney Hammond turns her focus to a Christian's most important relationship—with the Father.

A LADDER OUT OF DEPRESSION
by Bonnie Keen

Singer and author Bonnie Keen shares from personal experience about how to avoid misconceptions about depression, pray through doubt, seek spiritual and professional support, and emerge from the darkness to the light of hope.

THE PRAYER THAT CHANGES EVERYTHING®
by Stormie Omartian

Bestselling author Stormie Omartian shares personal stories, biblical truths, and practical guiding principles to reveal the wonders that take place when Christians offer praise in the middle of difficulties, sorrow, fear, and, yes, abundance and joy.

HARVEST HOUSE
PUBLISHERS